Spoonface
STEINBERG
and other plays

LEE HALL was born and brought up in Newcastle upon Tyne. He studied at Cambridge University and then worked in youth theatre. *I Luv You Jimmy Spud* won the 1996 Sony Award for new writing, the Richard Imison Award and the Alfred Bradley Bursary Award, and is soon to be shot as a feature film. He has written several other plays for radio and his first screenplay, *The Prince of Hearts,* will be broadcast on BBC 1.

S p o o n f a c e STEINBERG
and other plays
from Radio 4's GOD'S COUNTRY

by Lee Hall

BBC Books

To Erin

All the plays in this book were produced by Kate Rowland for
BBC Radio North and transmitted on Radio 4

ISBN 0 563 38398 4

First published in Great Britain in 1997

Published by BBC Books, an imprint of
BBC Worldwide Limited,
Woodlands, 80 Wood Lane, London W12 0TT

Designed by Tim Higgins

Set in Adobe Bembo

Printed in Great Britain by Martins the Printers Limited,
Berwick upon Tweed

Bound by Hunter and Foulis Limited, Edinburgh

Jacket printed by Belmont Press Limited, Northampton

Contents

Acknowledgements

My thanks to Gus, Michael, Hayley, Kulwant and Becky who gave
extraordinary performances, and to all the actors for being marvellous;
to everyone at BBC North in Manchester for their indefatigable labours;
to Stephen Quilley for allowing me to be writer-in-residence; to Joe
Ging for his faith, warmth and humour he is sorely missed; to Rod Hall
and Clare Barker for their guidance and friendship; to the memory
of Alfred Bradley and Richard Imison whose legacies gave me much-
needed support; to Erin Wilson for her endless intelligence, inspiration
and encouragement; to Harvey, an exemplary landlord; and to my family
and friends for their special forbearance, particularly Mam and Dad
to whom I am ever in debt.

Finally, special thanks to Kate Rowland whose vision, patience,
heedless hospitality and total expertise made work an absolute
pleasure.

LH

Introduction

GOD'S COUNTRY started in 1993 when I met Kate Rowland, then a radio drama producer at BBC North in Manchester. I gave her a play of mine to read and, although she didn't think it suitable for broadcast, she felt I was a writer worthy of a commission for Radio 4. I put together an idea about a boy called Jimmy Spud who thought he was a Geordie Ninja and set about writing it. I laboured over several drafts before realising it was hopeless – the play just didn't work. However, unlike TV or film where projects stay in 'development' for years without even the faintest chance of getting made, every radio commission comes with a production date and broadcast date. The first was looming large. I took to my bed in despair and was told in no uncertain terms by my girlfriend, Erin, that the play needed a big idea with some heart.

It looked like my writing career was over before it had begun. But, as I buried myself beneath the sheets, I suddenly had a vision, a glorious vision, which would snatch some victory from the jaws of defeat - a vision that Jimmy Spud was an angel. Within a couple of days I'd written a rough version. I showed this to Kate who thought it was much more promising and packed me off to Greenwich Village in New York, where I was then living, to finish the play properly. It was mid summer, the time when New Yorkers of any means leave the baked streets for the Hamptons, but instead I was stuck in a one-roomed studio with Erin and no money to fix the broken air-conditioner.

After much sweaty anguish, I finished the script with only days to go before the recording, jumped on a plane and arrived in Newcastle to face the actors and a long suffering Kate. She had borrowed a flat in which to do the recording and, within a couple of days, it was all over. I felt rather bamboozled by the whole experience, and still had no idea if what I'd written was any good. The script did make me laugh, but I thought this was probably a bad sign.

However, the reaction to the broadcast in February 1995 was very positive. Within a few months I had a deal to write the screenplay of *I Luv You Jimmy Spud*, within the year a mantelpiece full of awards. Such was the success of the play that Radio Drama asked if it could be developed into a series. I felt that Jimmy's story was complete in itself, but I had discovered the special freedom that using children's voices can have for a writer. The innocence, humour and irreverence a child's perspective can give you was something I wished to explore much more.

I was also surprised by the reaction to the theme of faith in Jimmy Spud. I had assumed this was all rather old fashioned and would be of no interest to anyone else, but to my surprise, it was the very thing that had attracted many people to the piece.

I decided that I would like to write a series which was loosely tied by Jimmy's presence but focused on other children dealing with faith in their own lives. And so the various stories emerged. *The Love Letters of Ragie Patel* is in many ways an update of L. P. Hartley's *The Go Between*. *The Sorrows of Sandra Saint* is about underage pregnancy, and *Spoonface Steinberg* is about death. All the plays attempt to weave pathos and humour inseparably.

The response to the individual plays has been remarkable, especially to *Spoonface Steinberg*. After many months I am still receiving letters about it. But whilst *Spoonface* obviously hit a chord, I see the plays as a complex whole. They are a collection of children's stories for adults. And in keeping with the best traditions of children's literature, it is the children who are wise and the grown ups who behave childishly. In the sentimental world of adulthood, children are repositories of innocence, but in the cruel world of children themselves, they are fighters, cynics, revolutionaries and bloody-minded pragmatists. Children are anything but innocent, anything but sentimental. That is not to say they aren't spiritual, ethical or moral beings, but anyone who has been a child will know they are incisive analysts of hypocrisy, failure and weakness, of almost any sort. They are not without compassion, but seldom make life easy.

Life, in these plays, is definitely not easy: people die, parents separate, they lose their jobs, they lose their marbles. Especially in the North, where the plays are set, even where things are booming we live in a culture of loss; a world of certainties that are falling away. The heavy industry which sustained a certain view of the world has been lost within a generation and with it has gone all the cultural and political signposts from which we take direction about our idea of ourselves. And it seems to me somewhere deep down we are all challenged to question our idea of faith. If industry cannot be our saviour, if some sort of municipal socialism won't miraculously create a utopia, and if God is dead, what are we to believe in? More fundamentally, what does believing actually mean?

What we do have left is a desperate pragmatism. We are all just trying to get through. But I firmly believe that it is precisely when we are trying to 'just get through' that we rely on resources which are spiritual in nature. And somewhere within every kale-eyed drunk, every hopeless destitute and long-suffering loser is a nobility that is impossible to extract from them being alive and being human. And whilst they may be mean and insufferable, there is still a resilience in them that is a common human thread.

Nobody seems to have this more than children. When I was researching *Spoonface Steinberg* I read that in many cases terminally ill kids were often able to counsel their parents through the last stages of their own deaths because they had come to terms with it themselves. This is not about innocence or supine acceptance, this is about maturity and understanding.

All this must sound very serious but in fact all these plays are comedies. They are old fashioned in many ways: unrepentantly sentimental but also desperately cynical. I am always striving to allow cack-handed lyricism to sit happily with slapstick bathos.

My intention is simply to provide some entertainment, and hopefully we can entertain as much with a good cry as with a good laugh.

Anyway, there are trainee angels, autistic girls who quote Kabbalistic theology and Boy Scouts who resurrect dead parents without even getting a badge. This is a world where the every-day brushes shoulders with the extraordinary; the mundane with the divine. In this way the stories are completely realistic, but realistic in the way children's stories are. Which is to say completely and not at all. It all depends on imagination, and it seems to me that if we can't believe in imagination we can't believe in very much at all.

LEE HALL
London, 1997

I Luv You Jimmy Spud

Characters

JIMMY SPUD   A boy
MAM   His mum
DAD   Her husband
GRANDDAD   Her father
SCOUT   A young boy
GABRIEL   An angel

The music in this play comes from Handel's *The Messiah*

I Love You Jimmy Spud was first performed on Radio 4 on 9 February 1995 with the following cast:

JIMMY SPUD   Gareth Brown
MAM   Charlie Hardwick
DAD/GABRIEL   Dave Whittaker
GRANDDAD   Joe Ging
SCOUT   Michael Walpert
Director   Kate Rowland

First Interview

Gabriel: Now just a few questions. All in your own good time.
　　The pass rate is seventy percent. Ready?

Jimmy: Erm.

Gabriel: OK?

Jimmy: Er, yes.

Gabriel: OK. I'll begin. General knowledge. Who was the first
　　President of the United States of America?

Jimmy: George Washington the first.

Gabriel: Where did Judas Iscariot kiss Jesus Christ?

Jimmy: Er?

Gabriel: I'm going to have to hurry you.

Jimmy: On the nose?

Gabriel: Gethsemene. Arithmetic. If it takes four men four hours
　　to dig a hole four feet by four feet, how long will it take two
　　men to dig the same hole, two by two?

Jimmy: One hour fifty minutes.

Gabriel: Theology. Does God exist?

Jimmy: Erm.

Gabriel: I'm going to have to hurry you on this one.

Jimmy: Yes. No. Pass.

Gabriel: Relativity. Which is lighter – a pound of feathers or a
　　pound of lead?

Jimmy: A pound of lead.

Gabriel: Which is better – to have loved and lost, or never to have
　　loved at all?

Jimmy: To love at all.

Gabriel: Which famous author on entering the United States of
　　America said, 'I have nothing to declare except my genius'?

Jimmy: Oscar Wilde.

Gabriel: Who put the bop in the bop showop de bop?

Jimmy: Rocky Sharpe and the Replays.

Gabriel: Is the redemption of the proletariat in Marx through
　　the transformative power of labour merely teleological mystifi-
　　cation or does it have real claims to a materialist theology?

Jimmy: Er, yes.
Gabriel: If I spat in your face would you turn the other cheek?
Jimmy: What?
Gabriel: Genealogy. Which came first – the chicken or the egg?
Jimmy: The egg.
Gabriel: The chicken. Eschatology. Does the contradiction in monotheistic systems of thought between agency and determination pose a problem for the notion of a redemptive afterlife?
Jimmy: Pass.
Gabriel: If you had all the money in the world what would you do?
Jimmy: Buy things and give the rest away.
Gabriel: If you had one wish what would it be?
Jimmy: Oh!?!
Gabriel: You are shipwrecked on a desert island. Which ten records would you choose to have with you? In descending order of preference.
Jimmy: Er, *Bohemian Rhapsody* by Freddie Mercury. Erm?
Gabriel: I'm going to have to hurry you.
Jimmy: That one by Ultravox.
   (The buzzer goes.)
Gabriel: Sorry, time up.
Jimmy: Can I go to the loo now?
Gabriel: You'll have to wait until the end of the assessment.
Jimmy: How did I do?

MUSIC: *'Glory To God' from* The Messiah

Home

(Throughout the scene the telly is burbling in the background. There is a sound of coughing.)

Jimmy: Do angels have girlfriends?
Dad: Oot the road, Jimmy.
Granddad: What's that, son?
Dad: Shift will ye?

Jimmy: Hey man, am deein' me exercises.

Dad: I'll exercise the back of me hand in a minute.

Mam: Jimmy, *The Dating Game* will be on soon.

Granddad: The opiate of the post industrial proletariat.

Jimmy: Is Priscilla Blank a slag Mam?

Mam: Where have you been hearing language like that?

Jimmy: Newhere.

Mam: Jimmy, you can't go round saying things like that, she's married with children.

Jimmy: Someone at school said it.

Mam: If someone at school jumped off the Tyne Bridge, would you?

Jimmy: No.

Mam: Well, you shouldn't go round saying things about Priscilla Blank. Do you want beans or peas with yer sausages?

Jimmy: But what's it mean?

Dad: Peas.

Mam: Never you mind.

Jimmy: Can I have beans Mam?

Mam: No you can't have ruddy beans. I'm not opening a whole tin for you.

Granddad: Jonathan Ross. Terry Wogan. Borgias of banality.

Dad: I'm not telling you again.

Jimmy: Granddad, what does polymorphous mean?

Mam: Oh, leave yer Granddad alone.

Jimmy: Why?

Dad: Shut it, Jimmy.

(Suddenly the voice from the television goes really loud. It's a Liverpudlian accent.)

TV (Priscilla): ... *Dawn from Luton got on with Brian from Dudley on a weekends' cross-country orienteering.*

Mam: Give uz the doofer, Dad. You'll deafen wi.

Granddad: What?

Jimmy: Priscilla Blank's cush isn't she?

Dad: She's bliddy murder.

Mam: You used to have her records.

Dad: So. Have ye seen the plight of her now?

Granddad: The expropriation of imaginative labour.

Mam: I bet you wouldn't mind half what she's earning.

Jimmy: You've turned it right down Granddad.

Dad: Bliddy Stalin, there.

Granddad: If ye'd spent less time watching this lot and more time working with yer comrades you might still have a bliddy job.

Dad: Give uz that doofer, here.

Granddad: Here catch. Look at the state of this lot.

Dad: It's the Addams Family outing.

Mam: Oh, she's all right though.

Dad: What! She's as rough as a bull's lug.

(The telly is turned up louder and they listen.)

TV (Contestant): *So as you can see I am a heavenly vision.*

Mam: What a load of codswallop.

TV (Contestant): *Which figure from popular cosmology are you? And how would you expand my spiritual horizons?*

Mam: De ye think these are scripted?

Dad: Wey aye man. Ye divvint think they mek it up on the spot do you?

TV (Priscilla): *Hello, Number Two.*

TV (Contestant): *I would be the angel Gabriel, because, baby, when the angel of the Lord comes you'll sure light up inside.*

(The crowd hoot approval.)

Jimmy: It's great this.

Granddad: It's a load of bliddy rubbish.

TV (Priscilla): *Number Three.*

TV (Contestant): *I'd have to be Lucifer because, baby, when I fall for you I fall a long long way, and where I'll end up it just gets hotter and hotter.*

Mam: She'll pick him.

Dad: But it didn't make sense.

Mam: It's not meant to make sense. It's just entertainment.

Dad: What's entertaining about watchin' these inbreds?

Mam: Look at the state of him.
   (Sounds of Dad and Granddad laughing and muttering.)
TV: ... *Contestant Number One.*
TV (Contestant): *Well, I would of course be Asmodeus, archdaemon of lechery.*
Mam: What a wally.
Dad: Where the hell do they get them?
Jimmy: What's lechery?
Dad: She's never picked him. He's a bleeding fruit.
Jimmy: What d'ye mean a fruit, Da?
Mam: Never you mind, Jimmy Spud.
Dad: Have you farted?

Second Interview

Gabriel: Name?
Jimmy: Jimmy Spud.
Gabriel: Date of birth?
Jimmy: Twentieth of the ninth, eighty-two.
Gabriel: Current occupation?
Jimmy: Schoolboy.
Gabriel: Any hereditary illnesses? Any formal debilities?
Jimmy: I had the mumps as a toddler.
Gabriel: Annual yearly income of household?
Jimmy: I don't know.
Gabriel: Just a ballpark figure.
Jimmy: I divvint knaa. Me Dad's on the dole and me Mam's a dinner lady.
Gabriel: Are your parents happy, Jimmy?
Jimmy: I divvint knaa. Me Dad's a right laugh.
Gabriel: But do you think they have a normal relationship?
Jimmy: I divvint knaa.
Gabriel: I'm just trying to get an overview, Jimmy. Nothing to get aggressive about. Did anyone ever touch you as a child. Do anything you didn't want to do?

Jimmy: Can I go to the toilet now?
Gabriel: We have to ask. It's standard procedure.

Home

Mam: *(Coming from the kitchen.)* Ergh! Have you let off?
Dad: What you on aboot? It's him.
Jimmy: Tell him Mam, it wasn't me.
Dad: Less of your backchat, son.
Jimmy: It must have been.
Dad: What are you on about? I never fart.
Mam: Divvint talk daft.
Granddad: The redistribution of wealth. That's the point.
Mam: The bairn doesn't want to hear this nonsense.
Jimmy: Mam, I do want to hear.
Dad: You listen to what yer Mam tells you.
Jimmy: Why? You never do.
Dad: I'll clip you in a minute.
    (Sound of Jimmy's lug being clipped.)
Jimmy: What was that for?
Dad: For being clever.
Jimmy: But I wasn't being clever.
Dad: I know, but ye thought ye were.
Jimmy: Ow!

Third Interview

Jimmy: ... and beans. And that bloke off the advert with the arm.
    And riding me bike. I love riding me bike.
Gabriel: Interesting. And what do you think are the most
    pernicious obstacles to leading a moral life?
Jimmy: What?
Gabriel: What do you think's really bad?
Jimmy: Er, tidying me room. Mr Bean – I hate Mr Bean.
Gabriel: Things that are really evil.

Jimmy: Er, I divvint knaa.

Gabriel: Think, Jimmy – things that are really evil.

Jimmy: What, like Hitler?

Gabriel: Why have you applied, Jimmy?

Jimmy: 'Cos it would be cush.

Gabriel: Cush?

Jimmy: To help babies and go around everywhere and that.

Gabriel: It would be cush?

Jimmy: I knaa.

Gabriel: Do you think you're ready for this?

Jimmy: Course. By the time people were my age in the olden days they were coalminers and that. Some of them had babies.

Gabriel: That's not strictly true.

Jimmy: Aw go on, though. Me Dad would be geet proud of uz.

Gabriel: But becoming an angel is a big responsibility.

Jimmy: I want responsibility. I want to make the world better and that.

Gabriel: It's not that simple.

Jimmy: Was that the wrong answer?

Gabriel: It's not a simple case of right and wrong.

Jimmy: But it must be, you're head of the angels.

Gabriel: Let me tell you, nothing's that simple anymore.

Jimmy: Oh!?

Home

Mam: It's like Casey's Court in here.

Jimmy: *(Going into the kitchen.)* Mam, Dad clipped uz for no reason.

Mam: I'll clip yer for no reason in a minute. Finish what you've got on yer plate.

Jimmy: I'm not hungry.

Dad: You're getting right on my wick.

Mam: Ey, what did the doctor say about that cough?

Dad: Oh it's nowt, man. I'm gannin to the Freeman for a check up.

Mam: It's that bliddy smoking.

Dad: It's just a cough.

Granddad: Paying to kill yersel.

Dad: It's the one bit iv pleasure I get in this house.

Granddad: It's always the same – would you listen about highrise housing? I predicted that back in the Sixties. But oh no, tek ne notice.

Dad: Look, I'm not sitting here with Chairman Mao ranting doon me lughole.

Mam: Where you going?

Dad: The club.

Mam: Well divvint come home pallatic.

Granddad: Here take me tickets for the meat draw.

(Dad goes out.)

Granddad: Can I have that last sausage?

Final Interview

Gabriel: I've given this some long and careful consideration and although your spiritual co-efficient has turned out surprisingly high your general knowledge has let you down.

Jimmy: What does that mean?

Gabriel: Well, it certainly rules out becoming a Seraphim. But I could make a special plea for a traineeship.

Jimmy: Aw thanks, like.

Gabriel: You realise this would be for a trial period only. If you prove yourself you get the halo no questions asked. If you screw up, I'm afraid it's game over.

Jimmy: Don't worry, I'll do me best.

Gabriel: I'll sort you out with the regular clobber – wings, all that stuff. OK?

Jimmy: Can I not have a harp?

Gabriel: I'm sorry?

Jimmy: A harp.

Gabriel: Reserved for cherubs, I'm afraid. But perhaps I could rustle up a trumpet or something.

Jimmy: Cush.

Gabriel: Here is a brief guide to the most important principles, but for the most part it's a question of thinking on your wings so to speak. OK?

Jimmy: Yes.

Gabriel: Well, do you have any other questions?

Jimmy: Where is Ulan Bator the capital of?

Gabriel: Sorry?

Jimmy: Ulan Bator.

Gabriel: Not that type of question.

Jimmy: It was a joke.

Gabriel: A theological one.

Jimmy: Well … I'd really like to know … well … does God exist?

Gabriel: You know I can't possibly say.

Jimmy: But you're the angel Gabriel.

Gabriel: Exactly. It's classified.

Jimmy: But isn't it important to know for sure?

Gabriel: Just be thankful for small mercies.

Jimmy: But how will I know if I've passed or not?

Gabriel: You'll know.

The House

(Dad comes home from the pub.
The sound of him singing as he comes through the front door.)

Mam: Yer stottin'.

Dad: I only had a couple iv halfs.

Granddad: What happened in the meat draw?

Dad: That Harry Nelson won a leg iv lamb.

Mam: Yer bladdered.

Dad: For the third time running.

Granddad: I reckon he knows somebody.

Mam: What's that you've got?

Dad: Where's the bairn?

Mam: He's in his room.

Dad: Now son. Come here.
Mam: Leave him be.
Dad: Jimmy.
Mam: It's half eleven.
Dad: Come here.
Jimmy: Hang on.
Granddad: It should be reported. You can't just stand by week after week.
Dad: Jimmy. Come here son, come here, come here. Now then listen, what have you always wanted, eh?
Jimmy: I divvint knaa.
Dad: Howay, man. Think.
Mam: Don't encourage him, Jimmy.
Granddad: The point is not to interpret the world.
Jimmy: A violin.
Dad: No man. Not a bloody violin.
Mam: Language.
Granddad: But to change it. Thesis on Feuerbach.
Mam: Granddad.
Jimmy: A dictionary.
Dad: Not a dictionary. What would any normal kid give their right arm for?
Jimmy: An organ?
Dad: An organ!
Jimmy: A tape deck? A chemistry kit? I divvint knaa. An encyclopedia?
Dad: A Gameboy.
Jimmy: Oh.
Dad: Look i.
Mam: Where did you get that?
Dad: Never mind. Open it.
Mam: It's knocked off, isn't it?
Dad: Nor, I bought it off your Trevor.
Mam: Well, it's definitely knocked off then.
Jimmy: Ta.

Mam: Give me that here.

Jimmy: Mam.

Dad: Is that all you can say? Eh, ta?

Mam: You can take it back where it came from.

Dad: Give the bairn back he's Gameboy.

Mam: Ower my dead body.

Dad: I've just bought it for him

Mam: I'm not having stolen property in this house.

Dad: Aye, what about the telly?

Mam: That's different.

Dad: Give the bairn he's Gameboy.

Granddad: Thieving bastards. I've been putting in to that draw for five years.

Mam: How did you pay for it?

Dad: Give him back the Gameboy.

Granddad: It's enough to turn you vegetarian.

Dad: Here son.

Jimmy: I divvint want it.

Dad: You're bloody well having it.

Mam: You swine.

Jimmy: I don't want a Gameboy.

Dad: I'll clag ye in a minute.

Mam: You ignorant sod.

Granddad: The point is to change all prevailing conditions. *Tabula rasa*. It's no good just rearranging the furniture you've got to knock down the house.

(Dad starts coughing terribly.)

Mam: You'll have to watch that cough.

Dad: I'm away to bed. Stuff the Gameboy.

Mam: Jimmy, what yer doing?

Jimmy: Just trying something out.

Mam: It looked like ye were floating in the air for a second.

Jimmy: Naw, it must have been yer imagination.

Mam: Night, night.

MUSIC: *'The Trumpet Shall Sound' from* The Messiah

Jimmy's Bedroom

Jimmy: Angel log. It's been geet boring at home the last few weeks.
All Dad does is cough he's guts up and all Mam does is get in
a nark. If I was Dad I would get a divorce. Come to think of it,
if I was Mam I would get a divorce in aal. If it carries on like
this I'm ganna get one where ye divorce yer Mam and Dad.
Then they'd be sorry. Also, I've been practising like mad.
And today I did something lush.

I was flying ower the toon looking down on aal the people.
All the poor beggars, and that, who ask for money ti buy
cider and aal the mams doing the shopping – to see if there was
anyone in need. But it started to pour with rain and I was
drenched and it was getting harder and harder to fly with the
wind's sworling. So I stopped on top iv Grey's Monument for a
breather but nebody saw uz 'cos I'm an Angel. And I was just
getting me puff back when I saw someone fall off their bike in
the distance, reet inti the river. And ne one noticed. So I flapped
along and swooped straight into the river with me gown on
and everything, like a dipper bird. And I grabbed him. But the
water's so horrible he'd passed oot and he was bigger than
me, I'm just little plus I'm just new at being an angel and there's
all this swirling like we were dancing but there was ne floor
and we had four left feet and I was twisting him up but he
was twisting me down and I couldn't hold me breath much
longer 'cos I was puffed from flying and suddenly I realised that
I was drowning inaal and me lungs started bursting and I was
all dizzy and wobbly, and it was pitch black and all I could feel
was this body I had me arms around and I was sinking down
and down and it was pitch black. Then all of a sudden we rushed
up like a gun going off and I burst up into the air, it tasted like
sherbet fountain. And we were both in the Tyne and the rain is
splashing little splishes everywhere: a million drips and we were
in the middle. And I see this beautiful boy scout with a hat
and alsorts, he's covered in gunk, so I quickly gave him the kiss
of life. And then he was even more beautiful when he came

round. And then he said: 'Bloody hell, you're an angel!' And
I said 'Yes. But I'm just a beginner.' And he said: 'Yer wearing a
dress.' And I said 'Yes, but divvint tell me Ma.' And I kissed
him again to make sure he was alreet. And we swum to the side.
He said he'd come round and show uz some knots that might
come in handy. Any road, life saving. That's like a guardian angel,
plus rescuing a scout is canny cush in itsel.

The House: Does God exist?

Jimmy: Mam.

Mam: What?

Jimmy: Mam, what if God does exist, but doesn't want ye to knaa
he does so he pretends he doesn't?

Mam: What, our Jimmy?

Jimmy: Well, what if he does exist and he's just pretending not to?

Mam: Oh, give it a rest Jimmy.

Jimmy: I mean he is God, so he can de what he wants.

Mam: Why don't you play with yer Gameboy?

Jimmy: I've been playing with me Gameboy. But if there isn't
a God and everybody thought there was a God but that he was
pretending that there wasn't one would that make any
difference?

Mam: Where've you been getting these ideas from?

Jimmy: I just thought iv them.

Mam: Look Jimmy, I'm not even religious so there's no point
asking me.

Jimmy: So there is ne God?

Mam: Well, how should I know?

(Dad comes in.)

Mam: It's not good, pet?

Jimmy: De ye think God exists, Dad?

Mam: Leave yer Dad alone.

Granddad: *(Coming in)* Yer a bit peaky, son.

Mam: Dad, he's just come back from the doctor's.

Jimmy: Granddad, you're an atheist, aren't you?

Granddad: Well, if there was a God why would there be war and disease and kids starving in Biafra and all that?

Jimmy: What's Biafra?

Dad: He means Rwanda, he's thirty year out iv date.

Mam: What did they say Peter?

Granddad: They're still starving in Biafra, it's on the telly.

Jimmy: So all the wars and that mean there's not a God?

Dad: I don't know.

Granddad: Well, if there was a God then he'd stop them, wouldn't he?

Jimmy: He might be busy.

Mam: Are you OK?

Jimmy: But can there still be miracles if there's ne God?

Mam: The only miracle round here will be you shutting up for sixty seconds.

Granddad: There's ne such thing as miracles, son.

Jimmy: But Granddad …

Granddad: Look i, Christianity's a right bliddy mess. For a start Jesus was a Jew.

Jimmy: Do Jews believe in God?

Dad: You'd have to ask a Jew.

Mam: Jimmy, stop asking these questions and set the table.

Jimmy: But I divvint knaa any Jews.

Mam: Ernie Winters and Schnorbitz.

Granddad: It's Bernie Winters, man.

(*Jimmy is setting the table rather noisily.*)

Mam: Bernie Winters, then. Peter?

Jimmy: How come God never had a wife?

Granddad: He never needed a wife. He's God, isn't he?

Jimmy: Wey how was Jesus born?

Mum: Stop asking stupid questions there's ne answer to.

Granddad: He slipped Mary a quickie.

Mum: Granddad.

Jimmy: Well what about Adam and Eve?

Dad: Will you shut up.

(*The clatter of knives and forks.*)

Jimmy: Ragie Patel sez that in Pakistan there's millions iv Gods.
And the have different arms and all sorts.

Granddad: Religion is the opiate of the masses, son.

Jimmy: So does that mean all the Gods don't exist or just some
of them?

Dad: I've warned you Jimmy. Everybody has different ways of
looking at things. So shut up.

Granddad: He was only asking a reasonable question.

Dad: Look i, I just want some peace and quiet.

Jimmy: It was a reasonable question.

Dad: Jimmy, go upstairs. I have to talk to yer Mam.

Granddad: You've got to let him think for himself.

Mam: What's the matter sweetheart?

Dad: Well, I got the X-rays and there was tumours all over
me left lung.

Granddad: Son …

Dad: If there is a bliddy God, what's he deing giving me cancer?

Jimmy: But if he does exist he'll probably save you.

Dad: Well somebody's going to have to.

Mam: Oh, Peter.

Dad: If you ask me, God is a bastard.

(*Sound of Dad going out and slamming the door.*)

Jimmy's Bedroom: Diary

Jimmy: Today I found out that the Devil is in fact an angel. In fact
he was one of the top angels. Weird, eh? So what happens if
I'm a bad angel and I don't know I am? I mean if the top angel
turns out to be the Devil what hope iv I got? It all seems
a bit strange if you ask me. Anyway, I suppose that's why I'm
only a trainee. Tomorrow I'm going to meet the scout I rescued.
I'm going to ask him if I can be his guardian angel. I bet that'd
impress them. It seems to me that this angel business is a bit

more complicated than I first reckoned. I thought it was just a case of flying about and doing some few good turns. Any road, I hope Dad gets better.

Bedtime

Mam: Jimmy, you should be asleep by now.
Jimmy: I am asleep
Mam: Jimmy.
   (Sounds of snoring from Jimmy. Mam opens the door to her bedroom and climbs into bed. We hear the scene from Jimmy's point of view, through the bedroom wall.)
Mam: Give uz a kiss, pet.
Dad: I divvint feel like it.
Mam: Come on, pet. You're gonna get better.
Dad: Yes.
Mam: Loads of people get better.
Dad: But you slowly suffocate.
Mam: You're not going to suffocate.
Dad: What'll you do?
Mam: Stop being morbid.
Dad: I'm not being morbid.
Mam: You are.
Dad: I'm worried about Jimmy.
Mam: Come on.
Dad: He's not normal.
Mam: Course he's normal.
Dad: He won't play football.
Mam: Is that all you can worry about whether Jimmy likes sports?
Dad: He's weird.
Mam: You're the one who's weird.
Dad: He needs a man's influence.
Mam: Sshh. And go to sleep now. Everything'll be fine.
   (Dad coughs.)

The Garden

Scout: Oh hello there, I'm over here.

Jimmy: How did you find it?

Scout: I recognised your dress.

Jimmy: Oh, this isn't the full wack. It's what angels wear on their time off. I was just sitting here out the way of me Mam and Dad.

Scout: I like gardens. Fancy a chip?

Jimmy: Thanks very much.

Scout: You must geet hungry with all that flying around.

Jimmy: Can I have another one?

Scout: Why don't you finish them.

Jimmy: I hope ye divvint think I'm a starver, like.

Scout: No. Anyway, ta for saving me life.

Jimmy: How's yer arm?

Scout: Alreet. I cannit get it right up here like I used to but ...

Jimmy: You just did.

Scout: What?

Jimmy: Get it up there.

Scout: I know it was a joke.

Jimmy: Aw.

Scout: That's a smashing bike you've got.

Jimmy: Ta.

Scout: I thought angels flew everywhere.

Jimmy: I knaa, but I'm just a learner.

Scout: Can I feel the tyres?

Jimmy: If you want to.

Scout I bet you have to be quite strong to get them up that much.

Jimmy: For us angels that's nowt.

Scout: Are angels strong, like?

Jimmy: Wey aye. Ye have to de physical fitness and all that.

Scout: I thought you'd be soft as clarts.

Jimmy: Feel me arms, man.

Scout: They're rock.

Jimmy: I knaa.

Scout: Are you really an angel?

Jimmy: Well, I'm deein' training.

Scout: I'm a scout you know.

Jimmy: Cush.

Scout: I bet scouts and angels have loads in common, don't they?

Jimmy: Well they both wear uniforms.

Scout: And they're always prepared.

Jimmy: I like yer toggle.

Scout: That's me woggle.

Jimmy: It's lush.

Scout: But do angels always wear dresses?

Jimmy: You don't think I'm cissy do ya?

Scout: Nor, it's cush.

Jimmy: Cush. Have ye seen these frills? – I added them mesel.

Scout: Have you saved lots of people?

Jimmy: No you're the only one so far.

Scout: Straights?

Jimmy: Well the first proper one.

Scout: Does your Dad know?

Jimmy: He's got cancer.

Scout: Oh.

Jimmy: Does your Dad know?

Scout: He's dead.

Jimmy: Oh … Are you lonely?

Scout: A bit.

Jimmy: Mebees I could be like, your guardian angel.

Scout: Honest?

Jimmy: It would help get uz accepted.

Scout: But are you lonely?

Jimmy: No.

Scout: But isn't it weird being an angel?

Jimmy: Uh uh.

Scout: But have you got any friends?

Jimmy: Not that many.

Scout: Does your Mam know?

Jimmy: No one really knows.
Scout: Will you be me guardian angel?
Jimmy: Promise not to tell anyone.
Scout: Not even Akela?
Jimmy: No.
Scout: OK.
Jimmy: How did your Dad die?
Scout: He got run over.
Jimmy: Oh.
Scout: Thanks for saving me life.
   (Scout kisses Jimmy.)
Scout: Was it alright to kiss you?
Jimmy: It's supposed to be good for you. Kissing angels.
Scout: Cush. Can I have a look at yer wings?
Jimmy: Well, I'm not sure if you should.
Scout: Go on. I'll not tell anybody.
Jimmy: Alreet. But'll have to take me top off.
Scout: Well, there's nebody looking.
Jimmy: There.
Scout: God. They're lush.
Jimmy: Course.
Scout: Can I feel them?
Jimmy: I don't know.
Scout: Just a little feel.
Jimmy: Gan on then.
Scout: They're like, sort iv soft.
Jimmy: Aren't they fluffy?
Scout: If I took my top off, would ye flap them on us?
Jimmy: Well, if ye want to.
Scout: Hang on … Go on then.
   (The sound of wings beating.)
Jimmy: Is that nice?
Scout: It tickles.
Jimmy: Do you like it?
Scout: It's good.

Jimmy: Tell uz when to stop.

Scout: Can't you do it any faster?

Jimmy: No man, I'd take off.

Scout: I wish I had wings inall.

Jimmy: I have to go in now.

Scout: Can you not stay out any longer?

Jimmy: Nor. Me Mam'll kill us.

Scout: Do angels get wrong?

Jimmy: All the time.

Scout: You'll come back though.

Jimmy: Divvint tell anyone ye touched me wings or I'll get in trouble.

Scout: I won't.

Jimmy: Mebees you'll help uz do some angel stuff through the week? I've got a celestial trumpet.

Scout: OK.

Jimmy: See you around then.

Scout: Bye.

(The backdoor slams.)

The House

MUSIC: *'The Hallelujah Chorus' from* The Messiah

Mam: What do you want for tea? Ah, do you have to play this music?

Jimmy: Just till the end of this side.

Granddad: So do you understand what I'm saying?

Dad: Give it a rest, Dad.

Granddad: But do you understand? It's the natural state of mankind to be equal and free.

Mam: Honestly Granddad, just give it a rest. What is this?

Jimmy: Handel.

Granddad: That old crank.

Mam: Turn it off.

Granddad: Did you get it?

Dad: For Christ sake.

Granddad: I'm going upstairs in that case.

(Sound of Granddad leaving.)

Mam: You upset him.

Dad: What Ho Chi Minh!

Mam: We could have fish fingers.

Dad: No, not the neet.

Mam: Or a pizza. I've got a frozen pizza here.

Dad: It's spread.

Mam: Cod steaks. They said it might spread even if it eventually gets better.

Dad: What about them pies, there? They need eating.

Mam: Pet, don't expect too much too soon. Turkey sausages?

Dad: Sod, the bliddy sausages.

Mam: Ah, pettle.

(Pause.)

Dad: Turn that bloody music off.

Jimmy: Mam.

Mam: Now.

(Pause. Jimmy turns it off and goes out slamming the door.)

Dad: Sorry.

Mam: It's all right, pet.

On the Stairs

Jimmy: What's the matter Granddad?

Granddad: Sssh.

Jimmy: Are you crying?

Granddad: No.

Jimmy: Why are you on the stairs?

Granddad: Just thinking.

Jimmy: They've hoyed uz oot.

Granddad: Sit here, son.

Jimmy: What'll happen?

Granddad: God knows.

Jimmy: Will he go to heaven?

Granddad: He's not dead yet. Let's not be too pessimistic.

Jimmy: OK.

Granddad: I know it's hard. You have to optimistic.

Jimmy: What's pessimistic?

Granddad: Optimism's seeing an opportunity in every disaster, pessimism is the reverse.

Jimmy: What are you?

Granddad: I don't know anymore. They're both just signs of being scared.

Jimmy: Isn't it right that if you believe in something enough you can make it happen?

Granddad: Maybe.

Jimmy: Granddad. Can I tell you a secret?

Granddad: Go on then.

Jimmy: I'm training to be an angel.

Granddad: That's nice.

Jimmy: Plus I have a friend that I have saved.

Granddad: Who's your friend?

Jimmy: A scout.

Granddad: Oh. I think ye can only ever really save yourself.

Jimmy: You won't tell anybody will you?

Granddad: You won't tell anybody that you saw me crying?

Jimmy: Not a soul.

Jimmy's Bedoom

(Sound of Dad coughing. Jimmy is playing his trumpet.)

Jimmy: I'm puffed.

Scout: Perhaps you should have a breather.

Jimmy: Do you think it'll make him better?

Scout: I don't really know.

Jimmy: Once I've practised maybes.

Scout: Would you play me a tune if I was ill?

Jimmy: Course … I found out that there are angels everywhere, you know.

Scout: Oh.

Jimmy: Even in Africa. The people there get something that a dead person wore and leave it out for the angels and the angels plant it and the dead person comes back to life.

Scout: Honest?

Jimmy: Straight up.

Scout: Maybes it's the heat.

Jimmy: I could try it for your Dad.

Scout: How?

Jimmy: Just get one of he's old shoes.

Scout: Alright.

Jimmy: I'll have another try.

(Jimmy carries on with his trumpet practice.)

Dad: Jimmy.

(Dad knocks on the door. Jimmy carries on with the trumpet.)

Dad: What's going on?

Jimmy: I'm practising.

Dad: Practising what?

Jimmy: Me celestial trumpet.

Dad: Yer what?

Jimmy: Cush, eh?

Dad: It's a bliddy racket.

Jimmy: It's music of the spheres, Dad.

Dad: What's he doing here?

Scout: Hello, Mr Spud.

Jimmy: Practising as well.

Dad: He hasn't even got a trumpet. Ey, I'm not having that carry on in here.

Jimmy: Tut.

Dad: Don't you tut me. Get outside if you want to make that kind iv racket. What have you got on?

Jimmy: Me tunic.

Dad: It's a frock, Jimmy.

Jimmy: Lush, eh?

Dad: It's a dress for Christ sake.

Jimmy: We added these bits wer sel.

Dad: I'll be the laughing stock.

Jimmy: It's just like spiritual overalls.

Dad: You take it off. You're not dressing like a fruit in this house.

Jimmy: Dad.

Dad: It's going the journey. Ye can play yer trumpet in jeans and a tee shirt like every bugger else.

Jimmy: But I've got to.

Dad: Off. Jesus. What's those things?

Jimmy: What?

Dad: Bristles.

Jimmy: They're new feathers coming through.

Dad: What have you been getting up to?

Jimmy: For wings.

Dad: Have you been sniffin glue?

Jimmy: There just growing in.

Dad: Did you stick them on our Jimmy?

Jimmy: No he didn't. It's natural.

Dad: Son, look i. This is not natural.

Jimmy: What's not natural?

Dad: You should know better, you're a scout.

Jimmy: But Dad ...

Dad: It's sick, man. Listen, you are banned in future.

Scout: Oh, Mr Spud.

Jimmy: What's he done wrong?

Dad: I'll tell your Akela. And don't pretend you don't know what all this is about.

Jimmy: What what's about?

Dad: You know fine well.

Jimmy: I don't know fine well.

Dad: You do know fine well.

Jimmy: I don't.

Dad: You lying little sod. You know fine well.

Jimmy: What?

Dad: Dresses.

Jimmy: *(Not understanding.)* Oh.

    (Pause.)

Dad: What did I ever do?

Jimmy: When?

Dad: When? When we brought you up decent, that's when.

Jimmy: Please, Dad. You're upset because of your cancer.

Dad: I'm not upset because of me cancer.

Jimmy: Yes you are.

Dad: No I'm not. Anyway I've got a good right to be upset.

    (Pause.) Has he been messing around with you?

Jimmy: What?

Dad: How old are yous?

Jimmy: I've become a beautiful angel, Dad.

Dad: You've become a little pervert.

Jimmy: I can fly, though.

Dad: It's disgusting.

Jimmy: No one knows.

Dad: I'm downstairs barely able to catch me breath and you're up
    here in a frock with a boy scout.

Jimmy: But if it wasn't natural how would I be it?

Dad: Natural! Natural! I'll show you bliddy natural. Give uz
    that ere.

Jimmy: Give uz that back. It's for to save you.

    (We hear the sound of Dad smashing the trumpet as he speaks.)

Jimmy: Don't smash it. Get off it.

Dad: Any more of this monkey business and it'll not be the
    soddin' trumpet that goes for a burton. Now do you under-
    stand lad?

Jimmy: You'll just be surprised because of the wonderment ...

    (Dad starts to cough really badly.)

Dad: You little bastard.

    (Dad still coughing. Mam comes in.)

Mam: What yer doing Jimmy?

Jimmy: He smashed up me celestial trumpet.

Mam: I'll smash yer ruddy heads together upsetting yer Dad
like that.

(Dad still coughing.)

Mam: Come on down stairs, luvver. And you put some clothes
on when you've got guests. It's alright.

(They go out.)

Scout: I don't think he likes me.

(Jimmy blows the trumpet. It makes a sad burp.)

Ruminations

Jimmy: September the first. Dad's cancer's getting worse. He
smashed up me celestial trumpet but I'm turning the other
cheek. Plus he won't let uz see Scout. Apparently cancer's a very
little thing that grows inside you like multiplying and you get
too full with it. Sometimes I feel there is a bigness inside iv me.
All sadness and littleness growing and multiplying into huge
spangliness. It's changed into all the goodness in the world
bursting to get out. And cancer is ticking like a little clock on a
bomb and all the bigness is there tickling till I'm sick. I divvint
kna how big the bigness gets before it bursts or how long the
cancer can go on. But to everyone else it's invisible. To everyone
else I'm invisible. But I think when the bigness bursts it'll burst
kisses and everyone will see the kisses and will kiss your eyes
like hummingbirds licking sweet little kisses on your eyes that
you can't tell are there, sly kisses chasing you down the street and
making you laugh and with the kisses on their lips and in their
ears and on their noses and that. No one will hate me 'cos
I'm an angel and no one'll hate angels anymore, they'll love the
angels and the kisses and everthing and I will be flying around
like hope. Everything will be better. At least, I think.

Jimmy's Garden

Scout: Here it is.

Jimmy: It's a sock.

Scout: I couldn't find a shoe.

Jimmy: Sssh.

Scout: What is it?

Jimmy: I thought I heard something.

Scout: Will it still work with a sock?

Jimmy: I divvint kna. Could you not find a shoe?

Scout: I've missed you.

Jimmy: Or a hat or something?

Scout: It's all there was.

Jimmy: I've missed you too. A sock.

Scout: Sorry.

Jimmy: Alright. Put it in.

Scout: Do you do a spell or something?

Jimmy: I'm an angel not a witch ye knaa.

Scout: Why didn't you come and see me Jimmy? Why?

Jimmy: Surrup. If me Dad hears he'll gan stotty.

Scout: I thought you were me guardian angel.

Jimmy: I still am. Ssssh … It's me Mam.

Scout: Oh no.

Jimmy: Try and hide.

Mam: Jimmy, what are you doing out here?

Jimmy: Just some gardening Mam.

Mam: It's four in the morning Jimmy.

Jimmy: I'm planting things.

Mam: What?

Jimmy: Socks and that.

Mam: Jimmy, you have to stop this, pet.

Jimmy: I'll not be long.

Mam: Don't be stupid.

Jimmy: It's not stupid. I'm planting dead souls.

Mam: Oh, I cannit cope, pet.

Jimmy: But you have to do it at night.

Mam: What are you doing here?
Jimmy: It's his Dad's sock.
Mam: And does you're Dad know about this?
Jimmy: He's dead.
Mam: Well, what about yer poor Mother?
Jimmy: He's a Scout, Mam.
Mam: Oh, look you'll have to go home now, son. Jimmy, get
to bed.
Jimmy: It's better than you can do.
Mam: Sssh. The neighbours.
Jimmy: Souls are like seeds, Mam.
Mam: Stop messing about.
Jimmy: Mam.
Mam: And give uz that spade.
Jimmy: Bye.
Scout: Bye.
   (We hear the sound of the backdoor slam.)

Home

Mam: Jimmy, sit down a minute there's something I need to
tell you.
Jimmy: Is it 'cos I woke you up?
Mam: No, it isn't, it's about yer Dad.
Jimmy: I'm sorry I was digging so loud.
Mam: Sshhh. You have to try and understand.
Jimmy: What's the matter?
Mam: They're going to take him in.
Jimmy: Where?
Mam: The hospice.
Jimmy: The hospice. He's pretty skinny.
Mam: Jimmy, that's because the tumour's growing.
Jimmy: Oh.
Mam: You know he won't come home.
Jimmy: He's going to live there for good?

Mam: Yes.

Jimmy: Are you going too?

Mam: He's gonna die, Jimmy.

Jimmy: That's why he's being so horrible innit?

Mam: Just forgive him for me.

Jimmy: I'm trying me best.

Mam: I know.

Jimmy: But he won't die Mam.

Mam: Jimmy, I know it's hard ...

Jimmy: But Mam, there is no death, really.

Mam: Jimmy.

Jimmy: You have to believe, I'll make him better

Mam: Shush, shush.

Jimmy: That's what angels do.

Mam: Jimmy, you're not a angel.

Jimmy: I am though.

Mam: You're not a angel. Listen.

Jimmy: I've been practising plus I've got wings.

Mam: This isn't easy for me.

Jimmy: I saved Scout. You have to believe.

Mam: Please, Jimmy.

Jimmy: No, Mam.

Mam: Dad's going to die. There's nothing anyone can do about it.

Jimmy: But the celestial powers ...

Mam: Shut up, Jimmy.

Jimmy: Listen to uz. *(Shouting)* They'll be no death.

Mam: Jimmy.

Jimmy: Believe it.

Mam: Be quiet.

Jimmy: No.

Mam: Listen.

Jimmy: No.

Mam: Yes. Yes. Yes. There is death.

Jimmy: No. No. No.

    (Mum slaps Jimmy to quieten him down.)

Mam: Oh, I'm sorry, pet.

Jimmy: You hit uz.

Mam: I didn't.

Jimmy: I hate you.

Mam: I didn't mean to.

Jimmy: You stupid cow.

Mam: Oh Jimmy!

Jimmy: I hate you.

Mam: Jimmy.

Jimmy: You smell of dog food.

Mam: I don't smell of dog food.

Jimmy: And cats' trays ...

Mam: Jimmy.

Jimmy: ... and monkies' bums and sheep's feet.

(Jimmy stops his reverie and listens to Mam crying for some time. He is shocked.)

Mam: I'm sorry Jimmy.

(Pause.)

Mam: I'm sorry.

Jimmy: You don't really smell of sheep's feet.

Mam: You're going to have to help me, Jimmy. You're going to have to be very grown up.

Jimmy: I'll try, Mam. Honest.

Mam: When we go and see yer Dad, you have to be on yer best behaviour. And when you see him, he's going to get worse and worse, the cancer makes you old and yellow, but you haven't got to say that to Dad.

Jimmy: Why not?

Mam: He doesn't know.

Jimmy: He doesn't know he's yellow?

Mam: He doesn't know he's going to die.

Jimmy: Oh?

Mam: Not for certain. We have to give him hope.

Jimmy: What for?

Mam: Give uz a cuddle Jimmy.

Jimmy: Do I have to?

Mam: Yes. Yes, you do. *(Whispers)* I love you, Jimmy Spud.
  OK. Now go on off to bed.

Jimmy: Night, night.

  (Jimmy closes the door and goes upstairs.)

Granddad: Jimmy.

Jimmy: Are you crying again?

Granddad: No. Look.

Jimmy: What is it?

Granddad: It was Grandma's dad's.

Jimmy: A trumpet.

Granddad: He used to play for Harry Roy.

Jimmy: Who?

Granddad: Don't tell anybody.

Jimmy: Granddad. You'll leave uz one of yer shoes won't you?

Granddad: Go to bed, son. Night, night.

From Bad to Worse

Jimmy: Things are going from bad to worse. Everything I do goes wrong but I have my special friend Scout and we have been practising for to make Dad better. I'm glad of Scout, he makes uz feel good. But I'm feeling weird and small, like when you look at the stars and they are a million years old and everything is slowly dying away and falling away and yer falling and there's no one to catch you and there you are just tiny and insignificant and yer rattling round infinity and there's no one to catch you and yer falling and there is almost no sound and if all of the history of the world was a beach, you are smaller than the smallest speck of sand dust and yer tumbling and there are no wings to save you and yer all alone. Plus the Gameboy broke. Least there are small mercies.

The Hospital

Jimmy: You might get a shock.

Scout: Why? – is he ugly?

Jimmy: Mam says you haven't got to mention it.

Scout: OK.

Jimmy: And if he throws a wobbler just keep going. It's for his own good.

Scout: Are you sure this is a good idea, man?

Jimmy: Look, he's asleep.

Scout: He looks terrible.

Jimmy: It's redemption. Dad, Dad.

Dad: Hello, son.

Jimmy: Are you alright?

Dad: Smashing.

Jimmy: Oh. Have you been out of bed today?

Dad: I walked down the corridor.

Jimmy: Cush.

Dad: I was puffed, like.

Jimmy: I bet you were.

(Dad coughs.)

Jimmy: Ye'll be deing kick boxing next.

Dad: Pass the mask.

Jimmy: Can I try it?

Dad: It's for if you're sick. *(He takes deep breaths.)* Hey, stop kicking the bed.

Jimmy: How do you feel Dad?

(Dad is still taking deep inhalations of oxygen.)

Dad: Not so good.

Jimmy: I forgive you for smashing me trumpet.

Dad: Oh.

(Coughing – for a long time.)

Dad: So how have you been, son?

Jimmy: OK.

Dad: Oh.

Jimmy: How are ye?

Dad: Not so bad.

Jimmy: Good.

Dad: Well, not so good really. *(No response from Jimmy.)* They said that although it's getting worse there's a good chance it'll not go into the other lung. So that's good.

Jimmy: You look really old, Dad.

(Silence.)

Dad: I shouldn't have done what I did.

Jimmy: It's alright.

Dad: It's only …

Jimmy: I know.

Dad: I love you.

Jimmy: Dad. Look who's here to see you.

Scout: Hello, Mr Spud.

Jimmy: I know you think it's weird.

Dad: Jesus.

Jimmy: But you have to let us try it out.

Dad: What?

Jimmy: We've been doing it for weeks.

Dad: Jimmy, yer only eleven.

Jimmy: I'm his guardian angel. And look a new trumpet.

(Dad breaks into a coughing fit.)

Dad: Oxygen.

(He takes deep breaths of oxygen from the mask.)

Jimmy: Divvint worry, you'll be alreet.

Dad: I've telt you about him Jimmy.

Jimmy: I'm an angel Dad, nowt'll happen.

Dad: Jimmy. Yer a deviant.

Jimmy: One day all cancer and stuff will be smashed into a million bits. And death and hell will be cast into a lake of fire. And we'll live in a new heaven and new earth, and things'll be cushdy. And God'll come and wipe away all the tears from our eyes, and there'll be no more sorrow, crying, pain. And no night, plagues or evil.

Dad: Everybody's looking.

Jimmy: Are you ready?

Dad: Put it away.

Jimmy: We've been practising.

Dad: I'm warning you.

Jimmy: It'll make you feel better.

(Jimmy plays the trumpet and starts singing 'There is a Balm in Gilead'. Jimmy and Scout sing the gospel hymn with immense conviction, almost transcendentally. They finish with a flourish and there is silence apart from the coughing and the deep breathing of Dad taking oxygen.)

Scout: Jimmy, I think it's made him worse.

Jimmy: Mebees you shouldn't have come.

Dad: Get out, get out! And don't you dare come here again. And you, you keep away from our Jimmy, you little bastard.

(They leave and go down the corridor.)

Scout: You're supposed to be a guardian angel.

Jimmy: What could I say? I thought it would be good.

Scout: You're crap at being an angel.

Jimmy: I can't help it.

Scout: You can't do anything. That sock stuff was useless.

Jimmy: It was supposed to be a shoe.

Scout: I don't want you to be me angel anymore.

Jimmy: But think of all the laughs we've had.

Scout: They were boring.

Jimmy: Even me wings.

Scout: I was just pretending.

Jimmy: Don't get upset.

Scout: I'm not upset.

Jimmy: You are.

Scout: I've got a good right to be. You made uz look a right divvy.

Jimmy: No I never.

Scout: Your Dad called uz a bastard.

Jimmy: But I didn't do owt.

Scout: That's the point. You're not me guardian angel any more.

Jimmy: But …
Scout: And that's final.
Jimmy: Shit.
   (The sound of a door closing.)

Church: The Last Post

(Jimmy is playing the last post. He is up the belfry.)

Granddad: *(Below)* Jimmy, Jimmy!
   (Jimmy stops playing the tune.)
Granddad: Jimmy, grab hold of the ladder son. Oh Christ, it's
   a lang way up here.
Jimmy: What ye dein'?
Granddad: I've brought a pie.
Jimmy: What about yer back?
Granddad: Are ye alreet, son?
Jimmy: Aye.
Granddad: Oh.
Jimmy: Well, no.
Granddad: De ye want some pie?
Jimmy: No.
Granddad: *(Eating his)* Oh it's delicious. Are you upset?
Jimmy: No.
Granddad: Why not?
Jimmy: 'Cos.
Granddad: You haven't been to see your Dad.
Jimmy: I know.
Granddad: They said he mightn't last the weekend.
Jimmy: Why does he hate uz?
Granddad: He doesn't hate ye.
Jimmy: He does. When I have kids I wouldn't break their trumpet
   and shout at them.
Granddad: He's dying, Jimmy.
Jimmy: So?

Granddad: He's petrified. Think what it's like to be dead.

Jimmy: I can't.

Granddad: That's why.

Jimmy: If I had kids I'd help them be angels.

Granddad: Mebees you won't have kids.

Jimmy: Mebees.

Granddad: Where's yer friend?

Jimmy: He went away.

Granddad: Where?

Jimmy: Granddad, I'm crap at being an angel. I'll never be a proper one.

Granddad: Jimmy, you can only do yer best.

Jimmy: But me best is crap.

Granddad: I think yer trying too hard, son.

Jimmy: Granddad, what if God is just a bastard?

Granddad: Does it make any difference?

Jimmy: I don't know.

Granddad: If yer an angel you have to realise that things aren't perfect, that's the point of angels. You have to love them just the same. That's all you can do.

Jimmy: He told uz not to go back.

Granddad: If he told you to jump off the Tyne Bridge?

Jimmy: What if I'm unnatural?

Granddad: How can you be unnatural? You're just you.

Jimmy: But what about wars and murder and rapes and that? What about devils who were angels? What about badness? Some things aren't natural, Granddad. There must be some things that are good and some things that are bad and some things that are natural. Else there'd be no difference.

Granddad: Mebees, there is no difference.

Jimmy: I'm different. There has to be difference, else there'd be no angels. Angels are messengers, that's what it means. If there was no difference there'd be no point in havin' angels 'cos everything would be obvious.

Granddad: Nothing's obvious anymore.

Jimmy: That's why I need to rescue people.
Granddad: Individual salvation's just bourgeois sophistry, son.
Jimmy: But divvint you want to be salvated?
Granddad: Everybody does. That's the point.
Jimmy: I'm going to stay here with the wind.
Granddad: Just tell him that you love him. That's enough.
Jimmy: It's not enough, Granddad. I'm can't go and see him.
    I'm staying here.
Granddad: I'll leave the rest of the pie.
Jimmy: OK.
    (Granddad descends the ladder and closes the belfry door far below.)

The Hospital: Night

(There is the sound of snoring and wheezing.)

Jimmy: Dad.
Dad: Jimmy. It's midnight.
Jimmy: Sssshh. I had to see you.
Dad: I said I didn't want to see you.
Jimmy: Don't say that, Dad.
Dad: What are you doing here?
Jimmy: I came to tell you that … Oh nothing .
Dad: This is the last thing that I need.
Jimmy: I came to tell you I still love you. *(Sound of wheezing.)*
    Honest.
Dad: I divvint knaa what's got into you.
Jimmy: Dad, I came to make it up.
Dad: All I want now is some peace and quiet, son.
Jimmy: Do you want me to go?
Dad: I want to get it over with.
Jimmy: Dad.
Dad: Do you understand?
Jimmy: All I ever wanted was to save you.
Dad: All you've done is embarrass uz, it's all anyone can do.

Jimmy: Please, Dad.

Dad: No.

Jimmy: I'm an angel, Dad. I was only trying.

Dad: Look … look man, there are no angels.

Jimmy: I was only trying.

Dad: All there is, is inevitable blackness.

Jimmy: But I tried.

Dad: What's the point?

Jimmy: Dad.

Dad: Put the pillow on me face.

Jimmy: I can't, they'll never accept uz.

Dad: Please.

Jimmy: Do you hate uz?

Dad: No, I love you.

Jimmy: I can't. I'm an angel.

Dad: Jimmy …

(The wheezing of Dad has got worse. But it suddenly becomes muffled as Jimmy suffocates his father.)

Jimmy: Dad? Dad? I need to explain. Why I'm different.

Dad. I'm not evil. I don't know if I'm good but.

I'm not evil.

I wouldn't do anything bad.

I came to turn the other cheek.

Dad. Dad.

Do you understand?

I can't do this.

Dad, I only wanted to make you better.

Wake up.

(The noise of his breathing has stopped.)

Shit. Shit.

Mam: Jimmy. You're here.

Jimmy: I was only trying, Mam.

Mam: It's alright, Jimmy. What did you do?

Jimmy: It's hopeless.

Mam: Jimmy.
Jimmy: He made uz.
Mam: Come here, son.
Jimmy: I'll never be an angel. Wake up.
Mam: He's gone, lover.
Jimmy: But I'll bring him back.
Mam: Jimmy.
Jimmy: Get off uz.
Mam: You're not an angel, Jimmy.
Jimmy: I am.
Mam: There's nothing we can do.
Jimmy: Wake up, you bastard.
Mam: Ssshhh.
Jimmy: It's got to work. *Hoc est corpus meum.*
Mam: Oh stop it.
Jimmy: It's what you say. *Hoc est corpus meum.*
Mam: Come 'ere baby.
Jimmy: Bastards. *Hoc est corpus meum* … Wake up.
Mam: Come with me.
Jimmy: It's got to work. Why doesn't it work?
Mam: We can't do everything we want to.
Jimmy: But I'm an angel.
Mam: Oh Jimmy.
Jimmy: Why won't it work? Why?
Mam: It's alright. I love you, Jimmy Spud.
Jimmy: *Hoc est corpus meum.*
　　(Jimmy starts to cry.)
Mam: It's all right. It's all right.
　　(A sudden rattling gasp from Dad.)
Dad: Christ, Jimmy. I thought I was a gonner there.
Jimmy: Dad.
Dad: And you know what I feel, right as bliddy rain.
Mam: Jimmy.
Dad: I love you Jimmy Spud.

TRIUMPHANT MUSIC: *'The Hallelujah Chorus'*
from The Messiah

Mam: Jimmy!
Dad: Jimmy?

The Transfiguration of Jimmy Spud

Jimmy: And I am light and all the light and my body is all rays and
the rays are love and I am love and I love who I want and
I am burning with words and I don't know if they are good
or bad words they are only love words and I'm bursting with kisses
humming bird kisses on the lips of the sick and the
lonely on the mean and the wretched the kisses are me and
I'm the kisses and I'm transformed as I transform you
and I am love as I love you all my body is rays.

MUSIC: *'The Hallelujah Chorus' from* The Messiah

THE END

The Love Letters of Ragie Patel

Characters

RAGIE PATEL A boy
JIMMY SPUD His friend
NANDINI Ragie's Auntie
GRANDDAD Ragie's Granddad
GRANDMA Ragie's Grandma
PAUL Nandini's boyfriend
RAMESH Her intended fiancée

The music in this play comes from *South Pacific*; music by
Richard Rodgers and lyrics by Oscar Hammerstein

The Love Letters of Ragie Patel was first performed
on Radio 4 on 6 January 1997 with the following cast:

RAGIE PATEL Kulwant Singh Bhatia
JIMMY Gareth Brown
NANDINI Nina Wadia
GRANDDAD Rashid Karapiet
GRANDMA Jamila Massey
PAUL Ralph Ineson
RAMESH Ravin J. Ganatra

Director Kate Rowland

MUSIC: *The Overture to* South Pacific

Letter

Ragie: *(Reading out loud)* Dear Dad, I'm sitting in my chair now. It's quite good only the legs are wobbly – so that's why the pen squiggles like that. First I was downstairs for a while, but then I came up here to write you a letter. You'll probably be in India by now, because of the time change. Any rate it is quite boring on account of everyone being on their holidays like you.

By the way, I don't hate you and Mum any more for making me stay here. I think it is because I am very mature now. When I'm old I will go on holiday as well and leave my children with you. Anyway, I hope you have a safe landing and I'll write to you everyday, or sometimes twice if I can get some extra paper.

Yours sincerely, Ragie Patel. (Your Son)

PS. Don't forget to look for some of them pointy shoes I was telling you about. I think you can get them at the market.

Ragie's Bedroom

Granddad: Ragie?
Ragie: Granddad.
Granddad: What are you doing up here?
Ragie: I'm writing a letter.
Granddad: He's only been gone forty minutes.
Ragie: Oh.
Granddad: Get yourself outside, it's a lovely day.
Ragie: I thought I'd stay here.
Granddad: I'm not having you moping around the house. I've got to go back down to the shop.
Ragie: Do I have to?

Granddad: You're just like your father. I hope you're not going to be insolent for the next six weeks.

Ragie: But I haven't been insolent. I'm only trying to be good.

Granddad: Well, get yourself some fresh air.

Ragie: OK.

Granddad: You might make yourself some new friends.

Ragie: What friends will I make round here?

Granddad: I don't know. Just get yourself out and see.

Ragie: But Granddad, I'm not very forthcoming in public situations.

Granddad: Look, just make sure you're back here sharpish for your tea.

The Back Lane

Jimmy: Excuse me. Do you believe in God?

Ragie: What do you mean?

Jimmy: Well, do you think he exists and that?

Ragie: God?

Jimmy: Yeah.

Ragie: I suppose so. Who are you?

Jimmy: So, what do you think he looks like?

Ragie: Well, there's different ones.

Jimmy: No there's not.

Ragie: There is in India.

Jimmy: Are you from India?

Ragie: No I'm from Durham.

Jimmy: Oh.

Ragie: But me Dad's from India. He's a doctor.

Jimmy: Straight.

Ragie: He went back though.

Jimmy: Has he left you, like?

Ragie: Just for the summer.

Jimmy: That must mean you're like an orphan.

Ragie: Not really. Maybes a temporary one.

Jimmy: I'm Jimmy Spud.

Ragie: Hello.

Jimmy: So in India they have different Gods to what we have?

Ragie: They've got loads of them.

Jimmy: What for?

Ragie: I don't know. One of them's got the head of an elephant and the body of a man.

Jimmy: With a trunk?

Ragie: And ears – the lot.

Jimmy: That's a bit weird.

Ragie: That's nowt. One of them's a monkey.

Jimmy: A monkey?

Ragie: And he had this mate who burnt his wife or something and she came out and wasn't even singed.

Jimmy: Out of a fire?

Ragie: Aye, that proved she was truthful. And there's all these other ones like Vishnu or something, he was a dwarf and then a wild boar.

Jimmy: Do you believe in it?

Ragie: I don't know.

Jimmy: It seems a bit weird to me that God is a dwarf.

Ragie: He wasn't just a dwarf you know.

Jimmy: What else was he?

Ragie: I don't know. Loads of things.

Jimmy: Well, how did you know he was a dwarf?

Ragie: Me Mam told me.

Jimmy: Does she believe in dwarves?

Ragie: No, but she says they are good stories. She's a teacher. But Dad says it's a load of old rubbish.

Jimmy: What, God?

Ragie: Everything. He says there's no such thing. But Granddad believes in them. He's got a model of the elephant gadgie in the house.

Jimmy: Do you reckon I could see it?

Ragie: I don't know. He's a bit weird.

Jimmy: The gadgie?

Ragie: No, Granddad.

Jimmy: Where does he live?

Ragie: Above the shop, just over there.

Jimmy: Is your Granddad Mr Patel?

Ragie: Why, like?

Jimmy: He's a right nutter, him.

Ragie: Is he?

Jimmy: He's got an axe under the counter you know. I seen him chase these lads with it.

Ragie: My Granddad?

Jimmy: He was running down the street with an axe. He's never chased you has he?

Ragie: Not yet. I've only been here since this morning. I hardly ever come because Dad and Granddad have these arguments.

Jimmy: He probably chased your Dad inall.

Ragie: It's quite hot isn't it?

Jimmy: So there isn't just one God but loads of them?

Ragie: I think there's hundreds but some of them are the same one twice.

Jimmy: How do you mean?

Ragie: Like in different shapes and stuff.

Jimmy: They change shape.

Ragie: More like change lives. They keep coming back. Everybody does. That's what Granddad reckons.

Jimmy: What? You come back after you're dead?

Ragie: That's reincarnation. Like after you die, then you come back as someone else.

Jimmy: Will I come back?

Ragie: Probably. You're probably someone else already.

Jimmy: Christ. Who do you think I am?

Ragie: I don't know. Will you stop asking me questions?

Jimmy: Why?

Ragie: I don't really know very much about this, you know.

Jimmy: But how will I find out who I really am?

Ragie: I don't know. You can get books on it.
Jimmy: Maybes I'll go to the library then.
Ragie: Look, I think I'd better go in now. It's nearly time for me tea.
Jimmy: Oh.
Ragie: Will you be my new friend while I'm here?
Jimmy: I suppose. What do Indians have for their tea?
Ragie: I don't know. Fish fingers or something.
Jimmy: I thought you'd have curry.
Ragie: I do sometimes. But I'm not really Indian you know.
Jimmy: What do you mean?
Ragie: I'm British.
Jimmy: But you look like an Indian.
Ragie: I know.
Jimmy: OK then. See you around.

MUSIC: *'Dites-Moi' from* South Pacific

The Kitchen

Ragie: Nandini. Do you like living here?
Nandini: Where?
Ragie: Here. With Granddad.
Nandini: I could think of better places to be.
Ragie: Where? I think he doesn't want me to be here.
Nandini: Of course he wants you to be here. It's just his way.
Ragie: Well, I can't help it if my Dad's dumped me.
Nandini: You'll just have to get used to him. He's not like your
    Dad, he's an old-fashioned patriarch.
Ragie: What's that?
Nandini: It's what they call it in Sociology.
Ragie: What's that?
Nandini: One of my A-Levels.
Ragie: You must be dead brainy.
Nandini: Not really.

Ragie: So you don't really like Granddad then?

Nandini: It's not a question whether I like him, Ragie. It's his attitude.

Ragie: Do you think he's evil?

Nandini: What are you on about?

Ragie: I heard he chased some people with an axe.

Nandini: Where have you been hearing things like that?

Ragie: Is it true?

Nandini: He chases people out of the shop if they're causing trouble.

Ragie: Well…

Nandini: It's not a question of being evil.

Ragie: But he believes in God, doesn't he?

Nandini: Well, that's debatable.

Ragie: But he's got one of them elephant men.

Nandini: It doesn't say he believes in it. I think it just makes him feel better to have it around. If you want to know the truth, Ragie, I think he does things because it's tradition. Not because he particularly believes in it.

Ragie: So you believe in it?

Nandini: Believe in what?

Ragie: Religion.

Nandini: Most of it's just superstition.

Ragie: Is that bad?

Nandini: If it forces you to do something just for the sake of it, yeah. You see, in religion everything's worked out in advance. Like fate.

Ragie: Do you believe in fate?

Nandini: I believe that we have to do certain things, but not in fate. I mean how would you change anything?

Ragie: What do you want to change?

Nandini: Anyway, I don't know why I'm telling you all this. You're not even interested.

Ragie: I am interested.

Nandini: Eat your dinner.

(Ragie stuffs some in his mouth.)

Ragie: Well, what about Grandma?

Nandini: What about Grandma?

Ragie: Do you like her?

Nandini: All she does is sit up there playing her stupid records …
her stupid musicals. *(Pause)*
Where did you go today?

Ragie: You know – just around.

Nandini: By the garage on the corner?

Ragie: I went everywhere. What would happen if the Gods really
do exist and you didn't believe in them?

Nandini: I don't know.

Ragie: Wouldn't you get in trouble?

Nandini: I don't think it would be very serious.

Ragie: What do you mean? That's the most serious kind of trouble
there is.

Nandini: Did you see anyone at the garage?

Ragie: No. Why?

Nandini: No reason. I just wondered, if I was to ask you a special
favour, could you be trusted?

Ragie: To do what?

Nandini: I need something to be delivered.

Ragie: Who to?

(Granddad enters.)

Granddad: Do you know your mother's up there shouting
for you.

Ragie: Who to?

Granddad: 'Who to' what?

Ragie: Nothing. I'll go and see her.

Granddad: But?

Nandini: Ragie.

Granddad: She's probably been shouting for the last half hour.
Why have you got this door shut?

Nandini: I don't know. Just by accident.

Granddad: She's shouting for her sweets.

Nandini: I'm sorry. Really, I didn't hear her.

Granddad: You're going to have to buck your ideas up young lady.

Nandini: Dad, I'm really sorry.

Granddad: You don't think this Ramesh from Manchester is going to put up with this kind of nonsense, do you?

Nandini: No, Dad.

Ragie: Who's Ramesh from Manchester?

Granddad: Who's Ramesh from Manchester?

Nandini: Dad.

Granddad: Didn't she tell you?

Ragie: Tell me what?

Granddad: He's Nandini's husband.

(Pause)

Ragie: Are you married?

Nandini: I'm going to be.

Ragie: To Ramesh?

Granddad: It's all arranged. You're invited.

Ragie: Me?

Granddad: Of course, your Dad'll miss it. But never mind, he probably wouldn't have come anyway.

Ragie: Why not?

Granddad: He says he doesn't believe in it.

Ragie: But he's married to my Mum.

Nandini: Arrangements, Ragie.

Ragie: Aren't you happy?

(Pause)

Nandini: Of course, I'm happy ... I'm just a bit nervous that's all.

Ragie: What of?

Nandini: Well, I haven't met him yet.

Granddad: He's coming up on Saturday to finalise everything. You'll see him then.

Ragie: You've never even met him?

Nandini: I've seen his picture.

Granddad: And you've talked to him quite a bit on the phone.

Ragie: Is he handsome?

Nandini: He's alright.
Granddad: He's a very attractive young man.
Grandma: *(Off)* Nandini!
Granddad: She's shouting.
Grandma: *(Off)* Where are my sweets? Nandini!
Granddad: Well …
Nandini: I was busy seeing to Ragie.
Grandma: *(Off)* Nandini!
Ragie: Granddad, can I go?

Grandma's Bedroom

(The words printed in italic in this scene are spoken in Gujarati)

Ragie: Grandma.
Grandma: *What is going on?*
Ragie: Grandma. It's me, Ragie.
Grandma: *Where are my sweets?* Where are my sweets?
Ragie: I've got your sweets here.
Grandma: Rag?
Ragie: No it's me, Ragie.
Grandma: Who are you?
Ragie: I'm your grandson. Remember?
Grandma: Oh.
Ragie: Ranjiv.
Grandma: Who?
Ragie: I've brought you some sweets.
Grandma: *You know the only thing in life is love.*
Ragie: Here.
Grandma: What's this?
Ragie: They're sweets. Granddad sent them.
Grandma: Who?
Ragie: Granddad.
Grandma: Rag?
Ragie: Grandma, I'm Ragie.

Grandma: Listen. I want to tell you something. It's a secret.
Promise not to tell anyone. Promise.
Ragie: OK.
Grandma: *They're all bastards.*
Ragie: What?
Grandma: *They're all bastards.*
Ragie: Say it in English, Grandma.
Grandma: They wish I was dead.
Ragie: Who does, Grandma?
Grandma: What?
Ragie: Who does? Who wishes you were dead?
Grandma: I don't know.
Ragie: I'll leave these here.
Grandma: Ragie, ask your Granddad to bring me some sweets.

MUSIC: *'Younger than Springtime' from* South Pacific

Ragie's Bedroom

(A knock at the door)

Nandini: It's only me.
Ragie: I was just getting ready for bed.
Nandini: Can I come in?
Ragie: Yeah.
(Nandini comes in and closes the door.)
Nandini: I brought you some sweets.
Ragie: Aren't they Grandma's?
Nandini: She gets enough.
Ragie: Do you not like Grandma?
Nandini: She's not the problem.
Ragie: Are you really going to get married?
Nandini: Supposedly.
Ragie: You must be quite old.
Nandini: Ranjiv, I'm only seventeen.

Ragie: Well, that's quite old. *(Pause)* Do you not want to marry him?

Nandini: I don't want to stay here. I mean, I asked them and everything.

Ragie: Asked them?

Nandini: To arrange it. But now it seems so sudden. I mean he's coming up at the weekend. We'll be married in a few weeks. I just didn't think things would turn out as they have.

Ragie: But aren't you pleased he got you a husband?

Nandini: I suppose.

Ragie: I thought you'd be glad. Most people want to get married, don't they?

Nandini: It's quite complicated.

Ragie: Is it …?

Nandini: I mean, what if I don't fall in love?

Ragie: But you have to love your husband, don't you?

Nandini: Not necessarily. You can't really help who you fall in love with.

Ragie: Can you fall in love with anybody?

Nandini: I suppose so.

Ragie: Even if they weren't your husband?

Nandini: Theoretically you could fall in love with anyone.

Ragie: What does it mean exactly – falling in love?

Nandini: You know, it's special. When someone makes you feel really nice.

Ragie: You mean when they're friendly?

Nandini: More than friendly. When you look at them, they should seem beautiful.

Ragie: Like you?

Nandini: Me?

Ragie: You're beautiful.

Nandini: Don't you think I'm fat?

Ragie: I think you're perfect.

Nandini: You're so sweet, Ragie Patel. *(She kisses him.)* Anyway, beauty's not just looks. It's the person inside that you fall in love with, don't you think? Their soul. I mean they could be anyone, but you see things that other people don't. I'm keeping you up.

Ragie: It's alright – I like being kept up.

Nandini: Ragie, if I give you this letter to deliver, will you promise not to tell anyone?

Ragie: A letter?

Nandini: Ssh.

Ragie: What's in it?

Nandini: It's personal.

Ragie: What's personal about it?

Nandini: If I tell you then it wouldn't be personal would it? Look, I'm asking you because this is very important.

Ragie: Who's it too?

Nandini: The man in the garage.

Ragie: The mechanic?

Nandini: Paul.

Ragie: You want me to give him a letter?

Nandini: Ssh. Yes.

Ragie: Why?

Nandini: Look, it's just to get some information.

Ragie: What for?

Nandini: A project.

Ragie: A project?

Nandini: At school.

Ragie: What about?

Nandini: What does it matter what it's about? Engines.

Ragie: Oh.

Nandini: For science.

Ragie: Oh.

Nandini: Look, just don't tell anyone.

Ragie: Why? Are you cheating?

Nandini: No.

Ragie: What if I get caught?

Nandini: You won't get caught.
Ragie: You might get expelled.
Nandini: I won't be expelled. Stop fussing.
Ragie: I don't want to do anything bad.
Nandini: You're not doing anything bad. You're doing something very important.
Ragie: Are you sure it will help your project?
Nandini: Positive.
Ragie: OK.
Nandini: Oh thank you.
   (She kisses him.)
Ragie: Nandini.
Nandini: Yes?
Ragie: I hope you do fall in love.
Nandini: Thank you, Ragie, thank you. Night, night.

MUSIC: *'There is Nothin' like a Dame' from* South Pacific

Letter

Ragie: Dear Dad, Today has been great success. First off I met a new friend, then I talked to Auntie Nandini. She is very beautiful and quite brainy. She is doing a project on pistons for sociology or something then she's going to get married to some bloke from Manchester who is very handsome, except she doesn't know if she is in love. I took Grandma some sweets and we had a good chat. Sometimes she thought I was Granddad, but never mind. Don't forget I am a size four and a half.

   Yours sincerely,

   Ragie Patel.

The Park

Jimmy: What do you reckon?

Ragie: It's quite big.

Jimmy: I got it from the library. I've nearly read it already. It's got all these pictures and that. Look there's the elephant gadgie.

Ragie: Cush isn't he?

Jimmy: He's quite fat.

Ragie: So would you be if you were an elephant.

Jimmy: It's says he wasn't an elephant until a witch came and chopped off his head and then they had to get him another one but all they could get was an elephant. It says he was quite handsome until he got his new head.

Ragie: Weird, eh?

Jimmy: There's all sorts in here. Look, there's a fella with four arms. They don't wear much.

Ragie: That's 'cos it's hot in India.

Jimmy: It's quite hot here.

Ragie: Who's that?

Jimmy: I thought you knew all about this.

Ragie: Not everything.

Jimmy: But aren't you a Hindu?

Ragie: Sort of.

Jimmy: What do you mean?

Ragie: You don't have to know everything to be a Hindu.

Jimmy: That's Indra

Ragie: What did he do?

Jimmy: I don't know. But it says here he has one thousand testicles.

Ragie: Oh.

Jimmy: Then it says that he had a fight and they covered him in vulvas.

Ragie: What's a vulva?

Jimmy: I don't know.

Ragie: Has it got a picture?

Jimmy: Just this 'un.

Ragie: He looks alright to me.

Jimmy: Maybe it was after he was cured.

Ragie: Was he cured like?

Jimmy: Apparently. You'd never have thought there'd be so many Gods in the world, would you?

Ragie: There's more than you think. You know that the Gods come down to earth all the time.

Jimmy: What do you mean, like?

Ragie: It's called incarnation or something. They come in the form of humans. See. Look at this one. He's just a little baby.

Jimmy: He's not a proper baby. He's got an old face.

Ragie: That's probably 'cos he's a God.

Jimmy: You know what? He looks like you.

Ragie: Do you think?

Jimmy: That's Vishnu. How would you know if you were an incarnation of a God?

Ragie: I don't know, you'd just know.

Jimmy: But what if you didn't know?

Ragie: Well, you'd be able to do miracles and that.

Jimmy: You know he looks dead like you.

Ragie: Do you think?

Jimmy: What if you're a God?

Ragie: Do you think I'm God-like?

Jimmy: You seem quite brainy.

Ragie: But not like a God.

Jimmy: Well, maybe you're just learning. Do you not think it would be cush being a God?

Ragie: Why?

Jimmy: 'Cos you could go around and help everybody and that.

Ragie: I suppose.

Jimmy: Plus everybody likes you. Look, there he is again and look, she's combing his hair.

Ragie: Who's that woman?

Jimmy: I don't know. Someone who fancies the God.

Ragie: People don't fancy Gods.

Jimmy: They do. I've read about it. They're always having children.

Ragie: Do you think people would fancy me if I was a God?

Jimmy: Probably. You're quite pretty.

Ragie: That woman looks like Nandini.

Jimmy: Who's Nandini?

Ragie: That's my aunt. She lives with Granddad.

Jimmy: Does she wear one of them dresses?

Ragie: A sari? No, mostly she wears jeans and that.

Jimmy: Do you think she fancies you?

Ragie: I don't know. She's getting married.

Jimmy: Ah.

Ragie: But I don't think she really wants to.

Jimmy: Why doesn't she want to get married?

Ragie: 'Cos she's never met her husband.

Jimmy: Well, maybes she was just saying that 'cos she was embarrassed.

Ragie: How do you mean?

Jimmy: Maybe she fancied you but she was too scared to say.

Ragie: Why would she be scared? She's a woman.

Jimmy: But what if she thinks you're a God?

Ragie: I never thought of that.

Jimmy: Do you fancy her?

Ragie: Who?

Jimmy: Your Auntie.

Ragie: No. I mean she's quite nice looking and everything.

Jimmy: But would you kiss her?

Ragie: I don't know. She kissed me.

Jimmy: She kissed you!

Ragie: The other night.

Jimmy: Where?

Ragie: In my bedroom. She came in and she kissed me.

Jimmy: Well she must fancy you then.

Ragie: Do you think?

Jimmy: It's obvious. She must think you're a God as well.

Ragie: A God?

Jimmy: Vishnu.

Ragie: Do you really think she likes me?

Jimmy: Why else would she kiss you?

Ragie: But what about her fiancée?

Jimmy: Maybe he doesn't really exist – I mean she's never even met him.

Ragie: I think you're reading too much into things.

Jimmy: Look, I have to go.

Ragie: Do you have to?

Jimmy: I'll come round tomorrow.

Ragie: Bring the book.

MUSIC: *'There is Nothin' like a Dame' from* South Pacific

The Garage

(The sound of a car revving up. It stops suddenly.)

Ragie: Hello.

Paul: Who the hell are you?

Ragie: I'm Ragie Patel.

Paul: Well, what are you doing underneath the car?

Ragie: I was trying to find you.

Paul: But I was in the back.

Ragie: I didn't know. I thought you were a mechanic.

Paul: I am.

Ragie: Well, I thought you'd be under here.

Paul: No, I was in the back. I think you better get yourself out now.

Ragie: Will you give me a hand?

Paul: Here.

Ragie: Look, I'm covered in gunk now.

Paul: Well, you shouldn't go crawling under people's cars then.

Ragie: Is this your garage?

Paul: No, I only work here.

Ragie: But you know about engines though?

Paul: Aye, a bit.

Ragie: But are you a specialist?

Paul: Well, to be honest, I don't really know a crankshaft from a big end, but I get by.

Ragie: Well, how do you fix the cars then?

Paul: Look, I get these books from the central library.

Ragie: Wow. Couldn't you get the sack?

Paul: The gaffer doesn't really care. He's a bit of a piss artist.

Ragie: An artist?

Paul: Well he's pallatic most of the time. Sometimes he's in the RVI. But I ... really I'm a poet.

Ragie: A poet?

Paul: It's not your traditional poetry. It's more stand up.

Ragie: Stand up poetry?

Paul: You know – in pubs and that.

Ragie: Won't your boss catch you?

Paul: He never goes in the Dog and Parrot.

Ragie: I brought you this.

Paul: What is it?

Ragie: It's a letter.

Paul: Who from?

Ragie: Nandini.

Paul: Nandini. *(Pause)* Did anyone see you come in?

Ragie: She wanted to know about pistons.

Paul: Pistons?

Ragie: For her project. *(The sound of Paul opening the letter.)* Do you mind if I ask you a question? What if someone's in love with you and you knew they shouldn't be?

Paul: What are you getting at?

Ragie: Well, I don't understand these things.

Paul: I think you should just mind your own business.

Ragie: I can't mind my own business. No one's ever fancied me before.

Paul: Who the hell fancies you?

Ragie: I can't tell you.

Paul: It's good if someone fancies you.

Ragie: But I don't think I want them to.
Paul: Why? Are they ugly?
Ragie: No, they're beautiful. But I think I'm too little.
Paul: Loads of people your age have girlfriends.
Ragie: Do they?
Paul: Of course.
Ragie: Do you think I'm special?
Paul: What do you mean? I've only just met you.
Ragie: I was just wondering.
Paul: Well, she must think you're special – letting you take these letters.
Ragie: Is taking letters special?
Paul: Course. You have fate in your hands, don't you?
Ragie: Do I?
Paul: Like Mercury.
Ragie: Who?
Paul: He was one of the Gods.
Ragie: How do you know that?
Paul: Well, I dunno.
Ragie: So what's it like?
Paul: What?
Ragie: Falling in love?
Paul: Well, it's very profound. Isn't it?
Ragie: Are you in love?
Paul: *(Pause)* Yes.
Ragie: With a girl?
Paul: Yes, with a girl. Are you not in love with a girl like?
Ragie: No.
Paul: Oh.
Ragie: More of a woman.
Paul: Well, that's even better. You just have to be confident.
Ragie: But I don't know how to be confident.
Paul: Don't worry. I wasn't very confident at your age. In fact I was a late developer. I never really had much self-esteem until I became a poet.

Ragie: But I'm not sure if she should love me at all really.

Paul: That makes it even better.

Ragie: Do you think?

Paul: Course, love conquers all, Ragie.

Ragie: Does it?

Paul: Look, if I just write down a reply will you give it to Nandini for me?

Ragie: I suppose so.

Paul: OK. *(He writes)* How do you spell 'delighted'?

Ragie: I thought you were a poet.

Paul: Well it's performance poetry, it's not writing it down.

MUSIC: *'A Cockeyed Optimist' from* South Pacific

The Living Room

Nandini: Ragie, this is Ramesh.

Ramesh: Very pleased to meet you.

Granddad: Ramesh's come all the way from Manchester.

Ragie: You came all that way?

Ramesh: I drove up this morning.

Ragie: Are you going to stay here?

Ramesh: No, I'm going back tonight. Just a flying visit.

Granddad: Ramesh is a very successful young man. He has his own business.

Ragie: You own a business?

Ramesh: Well, I'm starting one up. Cleaning carpets. I've been on a course and that.

Ragie: How do you mean? Cleaning carpets.

Ramesh: Well, you have a machine that injects boiling water into the pile and a hot water extraction device that sucks it up.

Ragie: But how do you get the carpet in it?

Ramesh: You don't put them in. You go over the top like a vacuum cleaner.

Ragie: Is that a business?

Ramesh: It's a start. When you think about it, if you can spend thirty pounds to get a room cleaned and it costs three hundred to have a new carpet, what would you do?

Ragie: I don't know.

Ramesh: Well, you'd spend the thirty pounds. It's obvious. There's a fortune in dirty feet.

Granddad: Ramesh was just telling Nandini how his parents will buy them a house.

Ramesh: They're going to put the deposit down.

Nandini: Where?

Ramesh: Longsight, I suppose.

Ragie: Where's that?

Ramesh: Near my parents.

Nandini: Manchester.

Ramesh: Of course.

Nandini: Oh.

Granddad: What's wrong with Manchester?

Ramesh: It's quite a nice place.

Nandini: It's just I don't know anybody in Manchester.

Ramesh: You'll know me.

Nandini: It's just that I hadn't thought I'd be moving away from here. You know, my friends and that.

Granddad: What friends do you have here?

Nandini: Don't know.

Ramesh: Look, why don't you and Mr Patel come for a visit?

Ragie: Can I come?

Nandini: What do you want to go for?

Ragie: To see what it's like.

Nandini: Look, stop complicating matters, Ragie.

Ramesh: No really. You'd be welcome. He could even come on his own.

Ragie: Honest?

Ramesh: After all you will be my new nephew.

Granddad: Isn't that nice.

Ragie: Cush.

Nandini: But what about college?

Ramesh: College?

Nandini: I thought I'd try and do a HND or something.

Ramesh: What do you want a HND for?

Nandini: To get a job.

Ramesh: But I thought you could work with me.

Nandini: Cleaning carpets?

Ramesh: No, you don't have to clean carpets. I thought you could do the paperwork. Mr Patel said you're doing business studies.

Nandini: It's just not what I was expecting.

Ramesh: Don't worry. I mean, I'm sure I could get you a job doing something else. My brother, he does desk-top publishing.

Nandini: Oh.

Granddad: You'll learn a damn sight more in business than going to college.

Ragie: Dad went to college.

Granddad: That was to be a doctor.

Nandini: So it's alright for him to go to college but not for me?

Granddad: But you don't want to be a doctor.

Nandini: What's that got to do with anything?

Granddad: You'll get better experience working with Ramesh and his brother.

Nandini: But I should have the opportunity.

Granddad: That's alright if you're an academic but what's the point of wasting time going to college if you're not very good. I mean you only got three GCSEs.

Nandini: Are you saying I'm thick, Dad?

Granddad: Course you're not thick. You're just not academic.

Ramesh: Anyway you can go to college in Manchester.

Ragie: You know when I come, can I go on the train?

Nandini: Ragie, you're not going to Manchester.

Ragie: But he said.

Granddad: Of course you can go.

Nandini: Shut up all of you. Dad, can you just leave us alone?

Granddad: What for?

Nandini: To get to know each other.
Granddad: But you've only just met.
Nandini: That's what I'm trying to tell you.

MUSIC: *'Happy Talk' from* South Pacific

The Park

Ramesh: I'm sorry about your Dad. I didn't mean this to get into
    some kind of argument.
Nandini: It wasn't your fault.
Ramesh: You know, it's quite weird for me as well.
Nandini: But you want to get married don't you?
Ramesh: Of course.
Nandini: Then why is it weird?
Ramesh: Well, I've never done it before.
Nandini: Do you believe in all this?
Ramesh: All what?
Nandini: Everything being arranged like this. You don't even
    know me.
Ramesh: Well, that's why I came up. To get to know you. Look,
    I don't want to make you do something you don't want to do.
Nandini: You're not making me do anything.
Ramesh: It's just … Well, there's plenty of people who get married
    because they think they're in love at eighteen or nineteen
    and then they're divorced by the time they're twenty-five. This
    way it's safer.
Nandini: Safer?
Ramesh: You know what you're getting into.
Nandini: But you might not even like me.
Ramesh: I do like you. I can see that already.
Nandini: You've only just met me. You don't know what I'm
    really like.
Ramesh: I can see you're a very nice person.
Nandini: You don't know that I am though, do you?

Ramesh: But you can get a feeling.

Nandini: But you can't tell what goes on in people's lives, can you?

Ramesh: Look, I'm not trying to be funny or anything. But you seem very special.

Nandini: What's special about me?

Ramesh: You're your own woman. I like that. And ...

Nandini: And?

Ramesh: You're very beautiful.

Nandini: Please.

Ramesh: Look, I wouldn't marry you just because I had to. I'd have to like you. And I think there's some chemistry between us.

Nandini: Chemistry?

Ramesh: Don't you think? Have you ever kissed anyone?

Nandini: A bit.

Ramesh: You know, I think you're gorgeous.

Nandini: Look, I don't know what I think about all this. I know you're a very decent man and everything. It's just ... didn't you ever want to fall in love properly?

Ramesh: There's different ways of falling in love. Look, just because I've come up here and I'm talking to your Dad and everything doesn't mean I'm some kind of nerd. I just want to make something of myself, with this business and that. I just want to do what's right.

Nandini: Don't you ever just want to do something wrong? Something bad for the sake of it.

Ramesh: What do you mean?

Nandini: Just to see how it feels. Just to find out what life must be like for other people.

Ramesh: I don't really care much about other people. *(Long pause)* Are you alright?

Nandini: I'm fine

Ramesh: It's just anyone would think that you didn't want to get married.

Nandini: I can't live here, can I? Dad can't afford college or anything, not with the mortgage on the shop and Mam.

Ramesh: Mam?

Nandini: She's not well.

Ramesh: I know this hasn't been easy for you. But you know, I think we're going to get on like a house on fire.

Nandini: I'm sorry I've been so awkward.

Ramesh: That's alright. So we're all set then?

Nandini: I suppose.

Ramesh: Well, I better be going. I'm supposed to be doing a three-piece suite tonight in Bolton.

MUSIC: *'I'm Gonna Wash That Man Right Out-a My Hair'* *from* South Pacific

Ragie's Bedroom

Ragie: I bet you're really glad now.

Nandini: What do you mean?

Ragie: That you're getting married.

Nandini: Why?

Ragie: He's quite handsome. Plus he's got a business and that.

Nandini: He hasn't got a business, all that he's got is a van.

Ragie: But he seems really nice and that.

Nandini: Oh, Ragie.

Ragie: He seemed alright to me.

Nandini: Ragie, you're only young. I'm the one who's got to marry him.

Ragie: So you don't want to get married at all?

Nandini: Not really.

Ragie: Does that mean I can't go to Manchester?

Nandini: Ragie, will you shut up about Manchester.

Ragie: But would you get married to someone else?

Nandini: Maybe.

Ragie: Who?

Nandini: Someone I really love.

Ragie: Are you in love with someone else?

Nandini: Stop asking questions.

Ragie: But there's someone you love?

Nandini: You're too young. It's just not right. I'm not in love.

Ragie: If you don't want to get married you should tell Granddad.

Nandini: I can't tell Dad, it's too complicated. He thinks he's doing the best thing for me. He wants me to be secure. He's got the debts from the shop plus he's got to look after my Mam.

Ragie: Perhaps you should just run away.

Nandini: Where would I go, Ragie?

Ragie: You could go to India.

Nandini: All I want is to go to college. To do a beauticians' course or something. Something useful. The last thing I want to do is to go to Manchester. I want to stay here.

Ragie: Why?

Nandini: To see what happens,

Ragie: What happens?

Nandini: If it all works out.

Ragie: But won't it be difficult. I mean the age difference.

Nandini: It's only a couple of years, Ragie.

Ragie: But what about Granddad?

Nandini: I don't know, it's all a bit scary.

Ragie: You're telling me.

Nandini: You're very special, Ragie.

Ragie: Thank you very much.

Nandini: For God's sake don't tell anyone about what we've been saying.

Ragie: I won't. And look I got those answers off Paul.

(Ragie hands over the letter.)

Nandini: Oh Ragie, you're a little angel.

(Nandini kisses him again.)

MUSIC: *'Bali Ha'i' from* South Pacific

The Back Lane

Jimmy: And she kissed you again?

Ragie: She said I was an angel.

Jimmy: See, what did I tell you.

Ragie: And she said that really she didn't want to get married to this fella from Manchester because she loved someone else.

Jimmy: Honest? Did she say anything else?

Ragie: I asked her who it was and she wouldn't tell me.

Jimmy: Well it must be you.

Ragie: Do you think?

Jimmy: She was probably embarrassed.

Ragie: Come to think of it she was blushing.

Jimmy: It's obvious. She wants to marry you instead.

Ragie: But I'm only ten.

Jimmy: Do you not want to marry her, like?

Ragie: I don't know if I'd be allowed.

Jimmy: I'd be sad if you got married.

Ragie: Why?

Jimmy: I wouldn't have anyone to talk to.

Ragie: I'd still talk to you if I got married.

Jimmy: I think you'd spend most of your time arguing.

Ragie: But do you really think she's in love with me?

Jimmy: It's obvious.

Ragie: What does it mean to be in love?

Jimmy: I think you feel all wobbly or something.

Ragie: Have you ever been in love?

Jimmy: I'm not sure.

Ragie: It's just I think Nandini shouldn't marry me. She should go with Ramesh. I mean how would I be able to afford it? I have to be at school.

Jimmy: You can get housing benefit and that. My Dad does.

Ragie: Jimmy, I think this is all a bit scary. What am I going to do?

Jimmy: You don't fancy her do you?

Ragie: *(Hesitates)* No.

Jimmy: Well, you have to tell her. That's being responsible.

Ragie: What should I say?

Jimmy: Just tell her that it would never work between you and that she needs someone more of her own age.

Ragie: But what if she takes no notice?

Jimmy: Maybe you should get married then.

Ragie: But don't you have to have sex and that?

Jimmy: I suppose so.

Ragie: But I won't know what to do.

Jimmy: You know, you can get books on it.

Ragie: Look, I've had enough of your bloody books. Look at the mess I'm in now.

Jimmy: It's nowt to do with the books. If it wasn't for me you wouldn't even know that any of this was going on.

Ragie: Look, I'm sorry.

Jimmy: Most people would be happy someone wanted to marry them.

Ragie: I have to go.

Jimmy: So do I.

Ragie: Did you ever find out what a vulva was?

Jimmy: I think it's a type of car.

Ragie: That's a Volvo.

Jimmy: Ah.

Ragie: Anyway, see you around.

Grandma's Bedroom

Ragie: Grandma, I've brought you some sweets.

Grandma: Is it raining again?

Ragie: No. It's quite hot. Why don't I open your curtains.

Grandma: Keep them closed. I can't stand the rain.

Ragie: But it's sunny.

Grandma: I said keep them closed. I hate this stupid country.

Ragie: You know in India – don't people get married when they're really young?

Grandma: Don't be ridiculous.

Ragie: But I thought sometimes they got married when they were nine or ten.

Grandma: It's the worst thing I ever did in my life.

Ragie: Do you wish you were still in India?

Grandma: Sometimes ... You're a good boy, you know that?

Ragie: I try my best.

Grandma: Give me the sweets.

Ragie: Grandma, I need to ask you a question.

Grandma: What my little angel?

Ragie: It's something I'm a bit confused about. I've been thinking about it all the time and I just don't know what the answer is.

Grandma: Oh ... You can tell me.

Ragie: I think Nandini wants to marry me.

Grandma: Nandini?

Ragie: I think she's fallen in love with me. She might even think I'm a God.

Grandma: Oh.

Ragie: Grandma, I don't know what to do.

Grandma: She's a very nice girl.

Ragie: But she's my Auntie.

Grandma: Who is?

Ragie: Nandini.

Grandma: Oh.

Ragie: So you think it's alright to get married then?

Grandma: Perfectly natural. I'm married, you know.

Ragie: I know.

Grandma: The worst thing I ever did.

Ragie: Can I ask something else?

Grandma: Go right ahead.

Ragie: Grandma, what's a vulva?

Grandma: What did you say?

Ragie: What is a vulva?

Grandma: Get out of this room.

Ragie: Please. I just wanna ...

Grandma: *(Shouting)* Just get out. Help! Nandini!

Ragie: Grandma.
Grandma: Nandini!
Ragie: You're spilling your sweets.
   (Nandini comes in.)
Nandini: What are you doing, Ragie?
Ragie: All I did was ask her a question.
Grandma: Get him away from me.
Nandini: Calm down, Mam. It's alright. Calm down.
Grandma: Get that child away from me.
Ragie: All I did was ask her a question.
Nandini: *(Shouting)* Get out!
   (Ragie goes out.)
Nandini: Calm down. What did he ask you?
   (Pause)
Grandma: I can't remember.

   MUSIC: *'Carefully Taught' from* South Pacific

Letter

Ragie: Dear Dad, I think you should try and come back as soon as
possible. There have been some terrible misunderstandings.
I think Auntie Nandini has fallen in love with me instead of her
husband Ramesh who runs a business. This is because I look
like one of them Gods in the book. Tomorrow she's taking me
to the coast. Please come home quickly so we can go back
to Durham, before Nandini tries to get me engaged.

   Yours sincerely, Ragie Patel.

   PS Please forget about the shoes. My friend Jimmy Spud
says that they are only made by children who get one penny per
shoe which is only enough to buy a papadam or something.
Please get me something made by adults at the going rate.

   PPS Please hurry.

Amusement Park

Ragie: Do you think it's right, me coming with you?

Nandini: Of course it is. It's perfectly natural.

Ragie: But isn't it a bit strange?

Nandini: Ragie, I think you should stop worrying about things so much.

Ragie: It's a bit weird with you being my Auntie.

Nandini: You have to stop seeing me as a relative.

Ragie: It's just a bit hard.

Nandini: You take things too seriously, Ragie.

Ragie: But you're supposed to be getting married.

Nandini: What's that got to do with anything?

Ragie: Well, don't you feel a bit worried about being in love with someone else?

Nandini: You can't help being in love. And anyway I don't feel anything for Ramesh. How can I? You've seen him.

Ragie: So you don't love him, even a bit?

Nandini: You can only love one person at a time. Look Ragie, you mustn't tell anyone about this.

Ragie: I think you should forget the whole thing. It's just not right.

Nandini: Sometimes what's supposed to be right and wrong doesn't matter – you just have to do what's in your heart. I'm sorry, I know you're a bit young for all this.

Ragie: But won't they go mad when they find out?

Nandini: Course they will. You just have to believe that we'll cope.

Ragie: We'll cope!?

Nandini: But you won't tell them yet though?

Ragie: But maybe this is a bad idea altogether. Maybe you should just go to Manchester and I could come on holidays.

Nandini: You don't understand. I'm not a child any more, Ragie. I'm not just going to do what people tell me. I'm a woman. I have needs. I have desires. God, I don't know why I'm telling you all this.

Ragie: Well, at least you're being honest.

Nandini: This isn't easy for me. I've never felt like this about anyone before.

Ragie: But isn't it unnatural?

Nandini: No. It's the most natural thing in the world.

Ragie: I feel a bit scared.

Nandini: Don't. It'll all work out, I think.

Ragie: Nandini, I … I think I love you too.

Nandini: Oh, you're so sweet. And I love you too, Ragie Patel.

Ragie: I feel embarrassed.

Nandini: Oh don't, don't feel embarrassed.

  (Nandini kisses Ragie.)

Nandini: Look, here's five pounds.

Ragie: You don't have to give me money.

Nandini: Please take it.

Ragie: I think it will spoil it if you start giving me money.

Nandini: You can play on the machines.

Ragie: The machines?

Nandini: You'd better stay here.

Ragie: Where are you going now?

Nandini: You understand how complicated this must be for me, don't you?

Ragie: It's complicated for me as well.

Nandini: I'll be back shortly. Just don't go anywhere.

Ragie: I'll be here waiting.

Nandini: Good.

Ragie: Are you sure you love me?

Nandini: Of course I am.

  M U S I C : *'Honey Bun' from* South Pacific

Tunnel of Love

Paul: I didn't think you were coming.

Nandini: It took me ages to persuade Ragie, and Dad was getting suspicious.

Paul: You look beautiful.

Nandini: Do you think?

Paul: You're gorgeous. *(They kiss.)* Oh, it's ridiculous. I work twenty feet from your back door and we've got to meet up miles away.

Nandini: I got your poem.

Paul: It should really be read out loud.

Nandini: I have read it out loud. I cried.

Paul: I've missed you.

Nandini: Me too.

Paul: You're gorgeous.

Nandini: He came up.

　(Pause)

Paul: What did you say?

Nandini: What could I say?

Paul: I can't go on like this. I sit in that garage and all day all I can do is look up and think of you sitting there. I swear I'm getting writer's block. It's ridiculous.

Nandini: You know I come when I can.

Paul: What are we going to do?

Nandini: I don't know.

Paul: Honest, I can't stand it. Look, I've been thinking – why don't you marry me?

Nandini: How on earth could I do that?

Paul: I don't know. We could just run off and go to the Civic Centre. You can get it done straight away.

Nandini: But that's impossible.

Paul: Not if you love me.

Nandini: I don't know if this is such a good idea.

Paul: You don't understand how much I love you, I would die for you.

Nandini: Really?

Paul: I would do anything. Remember – love conquers all.

Nandini: It's just all so sudden.

Paul: Just give me a few days to arrange it.

Nandini: Oh I don't know … I don't think this is a good idea.

Paul: Look, it's the only thing we can do.

Nandini: I suppose.
Paul: It's going to be alright. Honestly ... I love you, Nandini.
   (Long pause)
Nandini: I love you too.

   MUSIC: *'I'm in Love With a Wonderful Guy' from* South Pacific

Amusement Park

Nandini: Ragie.
Ragie: Are you alright?
Nandini: I'm fine.
Ragie: Where have you been?
Nandini: Nowhere.
Ragie: But you've been an hour.
Nandini: I had to sort something out.
Ragie: What?
Nandini: Just some arrangements.
Ragie: Arrangements?
Nandini: We're getting married.
   (Pause)
Ragie: Married? Do you think this is a good idea?
Nandini: I don't know, Ragie. It seems the only thing to do given
   the circumstances.
Ragie: But won't it be hard to do?
Nandini: Life's hard, Ragie.
Ragie: I know.
Nandini: We can't ruin our lives just because of what other people
   think. You've just got to say 'screw them'.
Ragie: Are you sure you won't get into trouble?
Nandini: Of course, we'll get in trouble.
Ragie: I'll get in trouble?
Nandini: Of course, you won't Ragie, it's my fault. I'll take
   the blame.
Ragie: So are you going to make all the arrangements?

Nandini: No, Paul will.
Ragie: Paul?
Nandini: He's going to sort it all out for us.
Ragie: Does he know a vicar?
Nandini: It's not going to be a religious marriage. We'll just go to the Civic Centre.
Ragie: Will I have to wear a suit?
Nandini: I'm not sure you should come, Ragie.
Ragie: I shouldn't come?
Nandini: Ragie, it's not a formal do. It's just to get a bit of paper.
Ragie: A bit of paper?
Nandini: That's all you need to be married.
Ragie: So I won't have to make a speech or anything?
Nandini: Don't worry, you won't have to do anything.
Ragie: Cush.
Nandini: Only you mustn't tell anybody. If anyone finds out beforehand ...
Ragie: Of course, I won't ... and you're sure it's allowed?
Nandini: I don't see how they can stop us.
Ragie: You know I really do love you, Nandini.
Nandini: I know, Ragie.
Ragie: But properly, not like a child.

MUSIC: *'Some Enchanted Evening' from* South Pacific

Letter

Ragie: Dear Dad, You know I sent you a note and everything about coming back. Well, now I think you should stay. It was all a bit of a mix up.

I am trying my best to be grown up here. So don't be surprised if I have changed a lot by the time you get back. But it's amazing how quickly people change when they are my age.

Your loving son, Ragie Patel.

Shop

Ragie: Granddad?

Granddad: Ragie, why don't you go out and play? I'm busy with these shelves.

Ragie: I was just wondering about Nandini.

Granddad: What about Nandini?

Ragie: Well, you want her to get married right?

Granddad: I should bloody well think so. Do you know how long it took to sort everything out?

Ragie: But would it really matter if it wasn't Ramesh?

Granddad: Well, who the hell else is going to marry her?

Ragie: But what if she wanted to marry someone else instead? That'd be alright wouldn't it?

Granddad: Of course, it wouldn't.

Ragie: Not even if they were quite nice?

Granddad: Are you trying to tell me something?

Ragie: No, I was only asking theoretically.

Granddad: Theoretically, if I found out someone was messing around with Nandini, I'd cripple the pair of them.

Ragie: Oh.

Granddad: Look, don't worry about the wedding. Nothing's going to stop it now. It's all arranged. Now bugger off, Ragie, I've got things to do.

Ragie: OK.

(As Ragie goes out the bell rings.)

Nandini's Room

Ragie: I'm terrified about all this.

Nandini: Calm down, Ragie. There's nothing to be scared of.

Ragie: But won't everybody get mad and that? What will my Dad say?

Nandini: I don't care what your Dad says.

Ragie: Are you not scared?

Nandini: Of course, I'm scared. I'm sort of excited at the
    same time.

Ragie: Are you?

Nandini: Well, it'll change everything. I mean, all my life I've
    looked out at other people seeing them do all these things. And
    at first I thought they were wrong for doing them, and then
    I realised that they were probably having fun. And now I realise
    there's all these possibilities.

Ragie: But aren't you scared about living together?

Nandini: Not really. I mean, we're in love aren't we?

Ragie: I suppose so.

Nandini: We're going to do it tonight.

Ragie: Do what?

Nandini: Get married. Paul's been down to the registry office,
    it's all sorted.

Ragie: Tonight!

Nandini: I guess it means I'll be free.

Ragie: You'll protect me from Granddad, won't you, if he starts to
    go mental?

Nandini: Of course I will Ragie. Look, will you take this down
    to Paul?

Ragie: What is it?

Nandini: It's just arrangements.

Ragie: OK … Nandini, do you know what a vulva is?

The Library

Ragie: And then she started talking about it.

Jimmy: Her thing?

Ragie: You know.

Jimmy: What did you do?

Ragie: I didn't know what to do.

Jimmy: I never knew it meant that.

Ragie: If I thought it was that, I wouldn't have asked her.
    Everything I do is a disaster.

Jimmy: Well, it can't be that bad. Grown up women don't talk to me about their thing.

Ragie: This is terrible. I was terrified in case she showed me it.

Jimmy: Wouldn't you want to see it?

Ragie: Not up close.

Jimmy: You might have liked it.

Ragie: But she's my Auntie. Plus, I don't think I'm ready yet.

Jimmy: What do you mean?

Ragie: What would Ramesh say?

Jimmy: Perhaps you should just go along with it and get married.

Ragie: Do you think?

Jimmy: Then it would be official.

Ragie: But what about poor Ramesh?

Jimmy: Would he be upset?

Ragie: He'd go mental.

Jimmy: Do you think?

Ragie: Especially since he invited me down there.

Jimmy: But if you don't want to marry her maybe she'll do something stupid.

Ragie: What would she do?

Jimmy: I don't know. She could do anything.

Ragie: This is terrible.

Jimmy: Maybe you should just tell Mr Patel and then he might just arrange something for you.

Ragie: But he wants Nandini to marry Ramesh because he's rich.

Jimmy: Is he rich?

Ragie: He's got a van and all sorts. Plus, Granddad said he'll cripple me.

Jimmy: Perhaps it's not such a good idea.

Ragie: Plus, I think Ramesh really loves her.

Jimmy: But do you love her?

(Long pause)

Ragie: Yes.

Jimmy: Really?

Ragie: What do you think's going to happen?

Jimmy: Don't know … I'm only eleven.

Ragie: Well, I'm only ten.

Jimmy: And she said you were going to get married tonight?

Ragie: It's all been arranged.

Jimmy: Did you do it?

Ragie: No. A mechanic.

Jimmy: Are you getting married by a mechanic?

Ragie: No, he's just sorted it out. Maybe he's getting one of them fancy cars for us.

Jimmy: It's a bit weird – a mechanic.

Ragie: What's weird about that?

Jimmy: Normally they have a best man to do all that.

Ragie: Well, I don't know any men do I?

Jimmy: You know me.

Ragie: You couldn't organise cars could you?

Jimmy: I would have a go. What's that?

Ragie: It's a letter.

Jimmy: *(Reading)* 'To Paul'.

Ragie: That's his name.

Jimmy: How does she know him in the first place?

Ragie: I don't know. He helps her with her homework.

Jimmy: Homework?

Ragie: On engines.

Jimmy: Nandini?

Ragie: Yeah. For science.

Jimmy: Smell the letter. It's weird – like flowers.

Ragie: I know they always do.

Jimmy: Does she send him lots of letters?

Ragie: All the time. She's doing a project.

Jimmy: How come she's doing a project when it's the holidays?

Ragie: I hadn't thought about that.

Jimmy: I don't think those letters were about engines.

Ragie: Well, what were they about?

Jimmy: You.

Ragie: Me?

Jimmy: I think she's been planning this marriage all along. I think you should open it.

Ragie: I don't think we should. What would Paul say?

Jimmy: He would never know. We can glue it back up again.

Ragie: But what if it's personal?

Jimmy: Ragie, man, it's personal to you. It's about your future. Give us it here.

(Jimmy opens the letter.)

Ragie: What does it say?

Jimmy: Wait a minute.

Ragie: Read it out.

Jimmy: 'Darling Paul, I need you so much. I think of you all day. I taste you. I smell you. I feel your hands all over my body.

Ragie: 'All over my body!'

Jimmy: 'I know now that I want to marry you.'

Ragie: I don't understand.

Jimmy: 'From the very bottom of my heart.' Christ!

Ragie: So she loves Paul as well.

Jimmy: I don't think she ever loved you at all.

Ragie: How's that?

Jimmy: I think we made a mistake.

Ragie: But he's only a mechanic.

Jimmy: Are you upset?

Ragie: Plus he's not even a proper mechanic either, he gets most of it out of books.

Jimmy: I thought you'd be happy.

Ragie: But I thought she loved me and everything.

Jimmy: Well, at least you won't have to marry her or anything.

Ragie: I hate her.

Jimmy: I thought you were scared to marry her anyway.

Ragie: How can she marry Paul, he isn't even Indian?

Jimmy: What's wrong with that? I'm not Indian.

Ragie: She'll probably want to marry you next.

Jimmy: Are you going to cry?

Ragie: I think we should put it back in the envelope.

Jimmy: Don't be too disappointed. I still like you.

Ragie: This is terrible.

Jimmy: Just think about poor Ramesh. Do you think he'll be upset?

Ragie: Course. She should be marrying him not that stupid bastard. I hate you.

Jimmy: What for? If it wasn't for me you'd have to marry her. You should be pleased.

Ragie: Pleased! This is all your fault.

Jimmy: How's it my fault?

Ragie: If I'd never opened the letter then everything would have been fine.

Jimmy: I was only trying to help.

Ragie: Wish I never knew now.

Jimmy: But it's best to know the truth, isn't it?

Ragie: If it wasn't for you, I would never have thought I was special in the first place. I would never have thought that Nandini fancied me.

Jimmy: But you only said she kissed you.

Ragie: She did, but how was I supposed to know it wasn't proper? She was just using me to take letters to that deformity.

Jimmy: I was just trying to be friendly.

Ragie: Well, you've ruined everything.

Jimmy: But I didn't do anything.

Ragie: I never want to see you again in my life.

Jimmy: But …

  (Ragie leaves.)

Jimmy: Wait! I'm sorry Ragie, what are you going to do?

Ragie: I don't know.

MUSIC: *'This Nearly Was Mine' from* South Pacific

The Garage

(The sound of an engine dying down.)

Paul: Ragie. Are you alright?
Ragie: Fine.
Paul: You just look a bit peaky.
Ragie: I am a bit peaky.
Paul: Why?
Ragie: I've had some bad news.
Paul: Bad news?
Ragie: It was quite upsetting.
Paul: You poor thing.
Ragie: It was about you.
Paul: What do you mean it was about me?
Ragie: I'm sorry.
Paul: What are you on about?
Ragie: She said that the wedding is off and she never wants to see you again.
Paul: She said that?
Ragie: She said she never really liked you in the first place, it was all a mistake.
Paul: But what about the baby?
Ragie: Baby …?
Paul: She didn't tell you?
Ragie: I don't understand.
Paul: Why do you think we're getting married?
Ragie: But …
Paul: Oh God, Ragie. I think I'm going to kill myself.
Ragie: Paul …
Paul: Oh, just get out, Ragie.
Ragie: I'm sorry.
Paul: Oh just go.
Ragie: I didn't know what I was doing.
Paul: Oh Jesus Christ!
Ragie: Please …
Paul: *(Shouting)* Get out and leave us alone Ragie!

Nandini's Room

Nandini: Ragie, what's the matter?

Ragie: Something's happened.

Nandini: Ragie.

Ragie: It's all been cancelled.

Nandini: Cancelled!

Ragie: I've done something awful. You see I thought you wanted to marry me.

Nandini: Marry you?

Ragie: I told him you never wanted to see him again. I never knew about the baby.

Nandini: You did what?

Ragie: I was upset, when I read the letter. I didn't know what I was doing.

Nandini: Ragie, what are you saying?

Grandma: *(Off)* Nandini!

Ragie: I thought you loved me.

Nandini: I don't understand.

Ragie: I thought when you were organising everything it was for me, that you thought I was a God. So I never gave him the letter. I just told him these lies.

Grandma: *(Off)* Nandini!

Nandini: Ragie!

Ragie: I'm sorry.

Nandini: You idiot!

Grandma: *(Off)* Nandini! I want you!

Ragie: I must have been jealous.

Nandini: Oh God, Ragie.

Grandma: *(Off)* Nandini!

(The door opens.)

Granddad: Nandini. What the hell are you two doing in here. Can't you hear she's shouting?

Ragie: Sorry Granddad.

Granddad: I thought I told you about mooching around the house.

Ragie: I was just going out.

Granddad: Well, off you go. And you, young woman, go and see your mother.

Grandma: *(Off)* Nandini!

(As Ragie goes out he drops the letter.)

Granddad: You've dropped something. Here ... who's Paul?

Ragie: Just someone.

Granddad: This isn't your writing.

(Granddad opens the letter.)

Ragie: Granddad.

(Long pause)

Granddad: OK young lady ... I think we need to have a talk with this young man of yours.

Ragie: But Granddad. You don't understand.

Granddad: Come with me you little slut.

Outside the Garage

(The garage door is shut and there's the sound of an engine running. Granddad bangs on the door.)

Granddad: Come on out. I know you're in there.

Ragie: Granddad.

Granddad: I'll smash this ruddy door in.

Nandini: Please, Dad.

Ragie: Granddad.

Granddad: I know you're in there. I can here that motor running ... I know you're in there.

Nandini: *(Sobbing hysterically)* Dad!

(The sound of Nandini sobbing fades.)

The Last Letter

Ragie: Dear Dad. I've been a bit better the last few days. I know Granddad sent you a proper letter explaining what happened. I can only write a little bit as the doctor said I was in shock or something. I have still not seen Nandini. She won't talk to anyone. Not even Ramesh who said he would marry her even though she'd had this affair.

When the ambulance got here poor Paul was still alive, but because of the fumes he was poisoned and died on the way to hospital. I never thought he'd really kill himself, only just be a bit upset. I think it is because he is a poet and everything.

Anyway, please come back soon. And remember all that stuff about how I was getting more mature? Well, really I still think I'm a child. Have a safe flight home.

Yours sincerely, Ragie Patel.

MUSIC: *'Some Enchanted Evening' from* South Pacific

THE END

Part 3 of GOD'S COUNTRY

The Sorrows
of Sandra Saint

Characters

SANDRA A girl
SCOUT (STEPHEN) Her brother
MAM Her mum

The Sorrows of Sandra Saint was first performed on
Radio 4 on 20 January 1997 with the following cast:

SANDRA Hayley Richardson
MAM Tracey Wilkinson
SCOUT Michael Walpert

Director Kate Rowland

Scout's Bedroom

Scout: Dad, if you can hear this. First, I hope you're alright and that. We miss you, you know that. And second, I just wanted to ask you, if there's any way of making Sandra be nice to uz, that would be very good indeed. She's always been quite horrible. But after what happened, she's been getting at uz like something rotten. That's all really. But, and I know this sounds daft and everything, if there's any way of coming back to see uz ... even for a bit ... well ... anyway, I have to go.

MUSIC: *'To Know Him is to Love Him' – The Teddy Bears*

Sandra's Bedroom

(The music fades, but plays under Sandra's next speech.)

Sandra: *(Reading)* What you may be feeling. Emotionally: instability comparable to pre-menstrual tension, irritability, mood swings, weepiness, misgivings, fear, joy, periodic elation, depression. Physically: fatigue, tiredness, frequent urination, occasional vomiting, heartburn, indigestion, food aversions, breast changes, amenorrhoea – absence of menstruation. *(Expostulating)* Jesus Christ!

(A few bars of music)

Scout's Bedroom

Scout: Do you miss him?
Sandra: Dad?
(Pause)
Scout: I mean do you talk to him?
Sandra: Don't be stupid.
Scout: It's not stupid. It's what the counsellor said.
Sandra: The counsellor?

Scout: It's supposed to help things.

Sandra: What's that going to help?

Scout: Coming to terms with it or something.

Sandra: It doesn't help anything.

Scout: I talk to him.

Sandra: Jesus Christ.

Scout: I knew you'd laugh.

Sandra: I wasn't laughing … What do you say?

Scout: I don't know. All sorts. What I've had for dinner, what's
   on telly. Normal stuff.

Sandra: What's on telly?

Scout: Well.

Sandra: He doesn't want to know what's on telly, man. He's dead.
   (Long pause)

Scout: I was only doing what they said.

Sandra: That's your trouble isn't it?

Scout: What's wrong with that?

Sandra: You end up talking to dead people for a start.

Scout: Well, I miss him.

Sandra: So do I, but it doesn't mean I have to delude myself.

Scout: But haven't I got a right to delude myself? I'm only twelve.

Sandra: Well, I'm only fourteen.

Scout: Well. There's a big difference.

Sandra: The difference is you won't face up to things.

Scout: Mam does it.

Sandra: Exactly.

Scout: At least I try.

Sandra: What's that meant to mean?

Scout: Mam says you need to get a hobby or something.

Sandra: Just because you're in the Scouts doesn't make you better
   than me.

Scout: I never said it did.

Sandra: You think you're king dick with all them badges.

Scout: It's not my fault I go to Scouts.

Sandra: Who's fault is it then?

Scout: You could go to Guides.
Sandra: I don't want to go to Guides.
Scout: Well, why are you complaining then?
Sandra: Just admit it. She hates me.
Scout: She doesn't hate you. She doesn't hate anyone.
Sandra: I'm not stupid.
Scout: Please Sandra.
Sandra: You hate uz.
Scout: How?
Sandra: The way you sit there and let me get picked on.
Scout: But I don't pick on you.
Sandra: You just sit there like a little smug bastard.
Scout: It's just the way I look.
Sandra: I'll tell you how you look. Like a crawling dick head.
Scout: I don't know why you're getting at me. He was my
    Dad too.
Sandra: I don't see why I have to get the blame.
Scout: But nobody's giving you the blame.
Sandra: I was the one who had to help him.
Scout: Don't.
Sandra: With all the blood and everything. And you and her
    sit there like butter wouldn't melt in your mouth.
Scout: If you hadn't have run out, he would have never got hit.
Sandra: So it *was* my fault?
    (Pause)
Scout: No. It was nobody's fault.
Sandra: Is that what Mam told you to say?
Scout: It's the truth.
Sandra: It's not what she thinks though.
Scout: Well, what do you expect?
Sandra: There. You see. It wasn't my fault I ran out. Things just
    happen. What if he had woke up the next day and got cancer,
    or fell down the stairs? Anything can happen. What if I had ran
    and nothing had been coming? But you have to gloat, don't
    you? You know what that is? *Schadenfreude.*

Scout: What does that mean?

Sandra: It means you take pleasure in other people's misfortune.

Scout: But that's what you do.

Sandra: I don't take pleasure. I'm just realistic.

Scout: I don't understand.

Sandra: I know you don't.

  (Pause)

Scout: What do you think happens when you die?

Sandra: Nothing.

Scout: So you think I should give up talking to him?

Sandra: Well, you can't bring him back to life.

Scout: Why are you so angry at everything.

Sandra: I'm not angry.

Scout: Oh.

Sandra: I just hate things that don't make sense.

Scout: Like Dad?

Sandra: Dad makes perfect sense. He had an accident and died.
  I mean people.

Scout: I don't know what you mean.

Sandra: That's your problem.

MUSIC: *'Come See About Me' – Diana Ross and The Supremes*

Sandra's Bedroom

Sandra: *(Reading)* Things you should do. In the first few months
  you will need a lot of emotional support. Feel free to share
  your feelings with people around you. If you feel worried
  or nervous be sure to talk to someone close to you. Avoid stress.
  Your body is out of balance. Try not to enter into situations
  or conversations that you normally find difficult. Take constant
  rests if you feel tired. If a nap at the office is not a reasonable
  goal, be sure there is a place you can sit and unwind undis-
  turbed. Let others baby you – perhaps your mother-in-law will
  do the ironing, perhaps your husband will take on some of
  the domestic duties.

The Kitchen

Mam: Would you like a biscuit? I just bought a packet.

Scout: What of?

Mam: Fig rolls.

Scout: But I hate fig rolls.

Mam: Where have they gone?

Scout: Why did you buy fig rolls?

Mam: I thought you liked them.

Scout: I hate them.

Mam: Well, that's news to me. You used to eat them.

Scout: Fig rolls?

Mam: Yes, fig rolls.

Scout: When?

Mam: All the time.

Scout: Sausage rolls.

Mam: What are you on about sausage rolls? I used to give you fig rolls when you went to camp.

Scout: Custard creams.

Mam: Custard creams?

Scout: You should get custard creams.

Mam: Where are they?

Scout: Where are what?

Mam: The fig rolls. They've disappeared.

Scout: But I don't want a fig roll.

Mam: Have you been eating them?

Scout: Mam.

Mam: It's Sandra, isn't it? I've told her.

Scout: Has she eaten them?

Mam: There was a whole packet here yesterday. Look.

(The sound of a tin being opened.)

Mam: There's nothing there. She'll blow up like a balloon. Where is she?

Scout: I don't know.

Mam: She's driving me round the twist.

Scout: I think she's at Karen's.

Mam: Maybe there's something I've done? Tell me. Is there
   something I've done?

Scout: I don't know.

Mam: What more can I do, Stephen?

Scout: Maybe she was hungry.

Mam: It's attention seeking. There was a whole packet in there.

Scout: Maybe she's bulimic.

Mam: She's not bulimic, she's a bloody menace.

Scout: It's only a packet of biscuits.

Mam: It's not the biscuits. It's her attitude. Take, take, take. Stephen,
   I'm doing everything I can. I'm at my rope's end.

Scout: Look, Mam, forget about the biscuits. I'll go to the shop,
   (The sound of the door opening. Sandra comes in.)

Mam: Here she is – Miss Biscuit.

Scout: Mam.

Mam: Where have you been?

Sandra: Out.

Mam: Where?

Sandra: Just about.

Mam: Have you been with that Karen Atkinson?

Sandra: We were doing our homework.

Mam: Till ten o'clock at night? *(Pause)* And what do you make
   of this?
   (The sound of a tin being opened.)

Sandra: Make of what?

Mam: This.

Sandra: It's empty.

Mam: Exactly.

Sandra: So?

Mam: Well, where did they go?

Sandra: What go?

Mam: The fig rolls.

Sandra: Fig rolls?

Mam: Don't play the innocent with me. I put them there
   yesterday.

Sandra: Fig rolls?

Mam: You ate the bloody lot of them.

Sandra: Mam, I don't even like fig rolls.

Mam: Well, there's a lot of people going off fig rolls all of a sudden.

Sandra: You never buy fig rolls.

Mam: Of course I do. I did yesterday.

Sandra: No, you didn't.

Mam: Don't you dare contradict me.

Sandra: I'm not contradicting you. I was here. I saw.

Mam: Saw what?

Sandra: Saw you never bought any biscuits. I'm going to bed.

Mam: Come here, young lady.

Sandra: What for? I'm not going to stand around arguing about biscuits you never bought.

Mam: Of course I bought them.

Sandra: Well, where are they then?

Mam: That's what I'm saying.

Sandra: Do you really think I'm going to eat a whole packet of fig rolls?

Mam: Well, what have you done with them?

Sandra: I haven't done anything.

Scout: But …

Sandra: *(To Scout)* Shut up, you.

Mam: I'm sure I bought them.

Sandra: You know what, Mam? You're doolally. You never bought any biscuits yesterday. You don't know what you're doing and then go round blaming people willy-nilly.

Mam: I do not blame people willy-nilly.

Sandra: Well, why are you on my back?

Mam: Because you go round acting like a selfish little cow.

Sandra: So that means I stole your biscuits?

Mam: I don't know what it means, Sandra, but it's got to stop.

Sandra: Well, it won't stop until you start being reasonable. You probably ate them yourself judging by the size of you.

Mam: Oh, get out.

Sandra: That's where I was going in the first place.

(To Scout) And wipe that smile off your face.

Scout: I haven't got a smile on my face.

Sandra: It's a good job as well.

(Sound of Sandra going out.)

Mam: I don't know what's got into her.

Scout: Mam, did you buy those biscuits?

(Long pause)

Mam: *(Unsure)* Course I did.

MUSIC: *Introduction to 'Back In My Arms Again' – Diana Ross and The Supremes*

Sandra's Bedroom

Sandra: *(Reading)* What to eat. The principles of nine months' healthy eating. *(She reads with gradually increasing horror.)* Every bite counts. Every meal you eat contributes to giving your child the best possible start in life. Remember now you are eating for two. To give your baby that kick start into health and happiness you must start eating a balanced diet.

Protein: four servings a day. Foods high in protein include nuts and seeds, whole grain baked goods, soy beans, yoghurt, hard-boiled eggs and wheatgerm. Vitamin C rich foods. Have at least two of the following: half a grapefruit, two small oranges, a half pound of shredded cabbage or a bowl of raw spinach. Whole grains and legumes, six to eleven servings per day: mung beans, millet, bulgar wheat, buckwheat groats, peas, butter beans or couscous. Bloody Hell!

MUSIC: *'Back In My Arms Again' – Diana Ross and The Supremes*

The Living Room

Mam: *(On the phone)* I am trying, Mam. It's ... you don't understand what she's like ... No, I am not making a mountain out of a mole hill ... You don't understand. I don't know what to do with her... All right, I will. I'll talk to her ... *(Getting irritated)* All right, I said I would talk to her ... Yes, OK. *(Sound of the door opening. Scout comes in.)* Jesus Christ! *(On the phone)* I have to go. *(To Scout)* What the hell's happened to you?

Scout: I fell in the river, Mam.

Mam: You're soaked. Are you all right?

Scout: I was pulled out by this lad. He said he was an angel.

Mam: You better get these clothes off. You're covered in gunk.

Scout: I know.

Mam: You didn't swallow anything did you?

Scout: I had my mouth shut.

Mam: What were you doing down by the river anyway?

Scout: Practising knots.

Mam: Well, I think you should stay home in future, sweetheart. *(She gets a towel.)* Here, let's dry you off.

Scout: Mam, do you still talk to Dad?

Mam: Sometimes.

(Pause)

Scout: He doesn't answer you though, does he?

Mam: Not in the normal sense.

Scout: Mam, do you think he can really hear?

Mam: I don't know, love. But there's no harm in trying.

Scout: I suppose so ... Mam, do you blame Sandra for what happened?

Mam: Of course I don't.

Scout: Do you hate her?

(Pause)

Mam: Of course, I don't hate her...it's just –

Scout: What?

Mam: I think you should go and get dry.

MUSIC: *'To Know Him Is To Love Him'* – *The Teddy Bears*

Sandra's Bedroom

(A knock on the door.)

Mam: Sandra, I've been thinking and I think we should talk.

Sandra: What about?

Mam: About this problem.

Sandra: What problem?

Mam: It doesn't have to be like this. I know I've been on edge – after what happened. And I realise that it hasn't been very easy for any of us.

Sandra: It's been quite simple for me.

Mam: Sandra, it can't be simple. Death isn't simple. You can't just shut off from it.

Sandra: That's what I'm trying to tell you. I'm not shut off from it, I've just come to terms with it.

Mam: But you go around as if you couldn't care less. It's not good for you.

Sandra: Don't tell me, what's good for uz. I'm the only one who's got over it.

Mam: You haven't got over it.

Sandra: Yes, I have. Because I don't feel guilty.

Mam: What's that meant to mean?

Sandra: Just what I said.

Mam: Guilty about what?

Sandra: For God's sake mother.

Mam: I come up here to make things easier for us and suddenly you go and start saying things like that.

Sandra: Well, it's true.

Mam: Nothing's true. What do you mean, guilty?

Sandra: It's true.

Mam: Well, everybody feels guilty. Some guilt.

Sandra: Not necessarily.

Mam: Well, they should. Everybody's a bit guilty.

Sandra: Here we go.

Mam: What do you mean?

Sandra: You just want someone else to blame. Someone to alleviate your shoulders.

Mam: You don't sound clever, you know.

Sandra: You think it was me, don't you?

(Slight pause)

Mam: I don't think it was anybody. *(Pause)* Sandra, I love you. You know that.

Sandra: Do you?

(Pause)

Mam: Of course I do. And the only way through this is to pull together and –

Sandra: And what?

Mam: Speak frankly.

Sandra: I am speaking frankly.

Mam: You're not, Sandra, all you're doing is going round in circles. You're picking at me. It's like this all day long. We all know how clever you are. You don't have to prove it by shooting everyone else down.

Sandra: Sorry.

Mam: Listen to you, you're not sorry.

Sandra: But you slept with that man, didn't you?

Mam: What man?

Sandra: In the office.

Mam: That has nothing to do with it.

Sandra: But it's true though.

Mam: It was years ago. It had nothing to do with you or Dad or Stephen or any of you. It was a mistake.

Sandra: You bet.

Mam: This is impossible.

Sandra: You know … the thing is … what you're trying to do … because everything in your life is out of control … everything is in chaos … you're trying to control us. You're trying to make us the perfect little things you'd like the world to be. And good little Stephen does his best, but I'm not living my life out for you.

Mam: I can't just let this go, the way you're behaving. *(Pause)* I think you're still grieving.

Sandra: So are you.

Mam: Of course I am.

Sandra: Do you think this started just because he died? Mam, I'm not a kid any more.

Mam: Oh, Sandra.

Sandra: Oh, Sandra what?

Mam: Why are you doing this?

Sandra: Doing what?

Mam: Pushing me.

Sandra: I'm not pushing anybody. You're pushing yourself.

Mam: I'm just trying to be reasonable.

Sandra: It's a bit late for that.

Mam: Do you know, anyone else would have thumped you by now.

Sandra: What's stopping you?

Mam: Oh, stop it.

Sandra: Stop what?

Mam: Oh, don't be ridiculous, Sandra.

Sandra: Go on, hit me. See what that would prove.

Mam: Oh shut up.

Sandra: Go on.

Mam: *(Screaming)* Oh stop it! Stop it! *(Calmer)* I don't want to have to shout at you. I don't want to have you hate me. I didn't want him to die. I don't want you to feel guilty. I don't want to force you into something. I don't want you to feel alone. Sandra, I've known you since you were a tiny child, and this is not you. For God's sake, I know I've screwed up enough over the last six months but surely you're intelligent enough to see I'm falling apart. You might think this is weird but I need you, Sandra. I need you. I can't lose you as well.
(Pause)

Sandra: Mam, I'm pregnant.
(Pause)

Mam: Don't be stupid.

(Slight pause)

Sandra: I'm not being stupid.

Mam: But what do you mean?

Sandra: I took a test. I'm late.

Mam: But...

Sandra: By two months.

(Long pause)

Mam: Oh my God – Why didn't you say any of this before?

Sandra: Say what?

Mam: Have you seen a doctor?

Sandra: How could I say something? I knew you'd go ballistic.

Mam: I'm not going ballistic. Am I?

Sandra: Look, you're starting.

Mam: I'm not starting anything.

Sandra: You never understand, do you?

Mam: I'm trying to understand. Sandra – you're fourteen.

Sandra: So?

Mam: Why didn't you use protection?

Sandra: It just happened.

Mam: Jesus Christ, Sandra. It doesn't just happen.

Sandra: Of course, it doesn't just happen. But it did happen.

Mam: Who's responsible?

Sandra: I am.

Mam: But who was the boy?

Sandra: What's that got to do with it?

Mam: Sandra.

Sandra: It could have been anybody.

Mam: Oh God, Sandra.

Sandra: You see? No wonder I haven't told you.

Mam: You have to tell me who it is.

Sandra: I don't know. I don't care. Do you think I want any of those poxy twerps having anything to do with it?

Mam: Twerps?

Sandra: I'm not having them bringing it up.

Mam: Bringing what up?
Sandra: The baby.
Mam: What baby?
Sandra: What baby do you think?
Mam: Sandra, there isn't going to be any baby.
Sandra: Mam, hasn't anybody explained the basic facts of human reproduction to you?
Mam: It's illegal. I mean –
Sandra: What?
Mam: You'll have to get rid of it.
Sandra: I'm not getting rid of anything. It's my life. It's my baby.
Mam: Sandra. This is a perfectly respectable household. Things like this don't happen.
Sandra: Oh?
Mam: You're acting like some slut from Walker.
Sandra: Why can they have babies and I shouldn't?.
Mam: They shouldn't be having babies either. Nobody should be having babies – nobody's gonna have babies. You're getting rid of it.
Sandra: See, you're going ballistic.
Mam: *(Ballistic)* I am not going ballistic.
Sandra: This is my choice – you've got nothing to do with it.
Mam: But you can have a child any time. You don't have to choose to have it now. You're too young Sandra. *(Pause)* You'll ruin your life.
Sandra: Did I ruin your life, then?
(Pause)
Mam: Sandra, I was twenty-three.
Sandra: What's that got to do with it?
Mam: You're not finished school. You haven't even done your mocks yet.
Sandra: I don't care about my mocks.
Mam: If you think having a baby's a way of getting out of your revision, you've got another think coming.
Sandra: I'll do them later.

Mam: You need to think this through.

Sandra: I have thought it through. When it goes to nursery, I'll do them at the college.

Mam: You haven't thought anything through. It's obvious.

Sandra: Because if I'd thought anything through, I'd get rid of it – what sort of argument's that?

Mam: A damn good one.

Sandra: It's not an argument. It's a plain assertion.

Mam: You're just a child.

Sandra: If I'm just a child, how the hell am I pregnant?

Mam: Oh, you're being ridiculous.

Sandra: That is not ridiculous. You just don't want to admit it.

Mam: Let's look at this objectively.

Sandra: OK.

Mam: Well …

Sandra: Well what?

Mam: If you have this child now you'll mess up the next few years at school.

Sandra: That's subjective.

Mam: It's not subjective.

Sandra: Yes it is.

Mam: You can't go to school.

Sandra: What about women with jobs?

Mam: Sandra.

Sandra: What about single mothers?

Mam: So you'd rather be a single mother on the dole for the rest of your life?

Sandra: Who's talking about the rest of my life? By the time I'm your age my child will have finished university.

Mam: You can't do this to me.

Sandra: I'm not doing anything to you. You're doing it to yourself.

Mam: I'm the only one who's going to be left looking after it.

Sandra: You don't have to do anything, if that's the way you feel.

Mam: That's not the way I feel.

Sandra: What do you feel?

Mam: Oh Jesus, I don't know.

Sandra: You know how stupid I am? There was part of uz that actually thought you might be pleased.

Mam: How could you think I could be happy?

Sandra: That there was life after Dad.

Mam: What's that got to do with it?

Sandra: That there's some hope, you know. That things don't have to stop. Like there's some bigger purpose than having to get on with domestic science or worrying about biscuits. I just thought there might be something. I thought you might realise you can't just plan things out neat, 'cos the world isn't like that, because there's more to life than just choosing a university, you know. Because you could wake up one morning and be run over by a bus. And if all you're worried about is how to pay the mortgage or that you wished you were better insured, well then you're already dead, Mam. Because life's about what you feel inside, life's about passions and caring for people, life's about creating things and moving on, not stopping them dead. Life's about saying screw you to the things that are trying to wring it out of you, life's about babies and having sex and hormones, a long time before GCSEs were invented or mortgages or child benefit. Life's wonderful and difficult and complicated.

Mam: You don't have any idea what life's about.

Sandra: What I hate about you, Mam, is that you brought us up on all of that bullshit and you never even believed a single word. Not a single word.

(Long pause)

Mam: I don't know what to say.

Sandra: You don't have to say anything.

(Pause)

Mam: What the hell would your Dad have said?

Sandra: That's price that is.

Mam: Sandra …

Sandra: He's dead, Mam. You never understood anything about him anyway.

Mam: Sandra.
Sandra: Not a single thing. He hated you, Mam.
Mam: He didn't hate me.
Sandra: He hated you, just like you hate me. Why don't you just
   admit it? *(Pause)* Go on admit it. *(Pause)* What's the matter
   with you?
Mam: I'm not going to admit anything.

> MUSIC: *'Stop! In The Name Of Love' – Diana Ross
> and The Supremes*

Sandra's Bedroom

Sandra: *(Reading)* The second month. Symptoms you may feel,
   sometimes individually, sometimes combined: periodic exhaus-
   tion, constipation, bloating, occasional faintness or dizziness,
   the tightening of clothes around the waist or abdomen probably
   due to bowel distension rather than uterine growth. At this
   stage the embryo is one and a quarter inches long. It has
   a beating heart, arms and legs with the beginning of fingers
   and toes.

Sandra's Bedroom

Scout: Are you really going to have a baby?
Sandra: Of course.
Scout: So I'll be like an uncle.
Sandra: You won't be 'like' anything. You'll be an uncle.
Scout: That'll be weird. Being an uncle and still being at school.
Sandra: There's plenty of people like that. You know Karen
   Atkinson. She's got three nephews.
Scout: Weird … Sandra, aren't you quite young to be having
   a baby?
Sandra: Jesus Christ.
Scout: I was only asking.

Sandra: By the time I have it I'll be in the fifth year.

Scout: Will you take it to school?

Sandra: Of course I won't take it to school. Can you imagine me sitting in Maths breast-feeding?

Scout: Will you breast-feed it?

Sandra: What did you think I was going to do?

Scout: I don't know.

Sandra: I'll have to stay with it for a while. Apparently they get a tutor in for you.

Scout: What to come here?

Sandra: Apparently.

Scout: So you'll just sit round here and get lessons without having to go to school?

Sandra: Yeah, I suppose.

Scout: I wish I could get pregnant.

Sandra: There's no fear of that.

Scout: I know. I've never even had sex. *(Pause)* Promise not to tell Mam, but I think it will be quite good fun.

Sandra: What will?

Scout: You know, having a baby here.

Sandra: Really? Do you think?

Scout: Well, I know they cry a lot and stuff, but you know.

Sandra: Listen, you haven't gone round telling everybody have you?

Scout: Who would I tell?

Sandra: One of your friends.

Scout: I haven't really got any friends. There's this one lad wants to be my guardian angel, but that's not a friend is it?

Sandra: Well, just keep it to yourself.

Scout: Why?

Sandra: It's illegal.

Scout: What? Having babies?

Sandra: Having sex. The person who is the baby's dad could be arrested.

Scout: Christ.

Sandra: I know.

Scout: Sandra, are you in trouble?

Sandra: I don't think I've done anything wrong. Do you?

Scout: I don't know. I don't think so. *(Pause)* Do you want a boy or a girl?

Sandra: I don't really care.

Scout: Really?

Sandra: A boy.

Scout: What would you call him?

Sandra: Alan.

Scout: After Dad?

Sandra: What's she doing?

Scout: She's still on the phone to Grandma. She was going eppy.

Sandra: She wasn't very happy when I told her.

Scout: You'd have thought she'd be pleased.

Sandra: You'd have thought.

  (Pause)

Scout: So you know, when like, you know, when you get pregnant … well, you have like, you know …

Sandra: What?

Scout: You know.

Sandra: Have sex.

Scout: Yes. *(Pause)* Well, what's it like?

Sandra: You can't ask me that. I'm your sister.

Scout: Why not?

Sandra: It's personal.

Scout: Well, who else am I going to ask?

Sandra: I don't know.

Scout: You're the only person I know who's had sex.

Sandra: What about Mam?

Scout: I'm not going to ask her am I?

Sandra: It's alright.

  (Pause)

Scout: Just alright?

Sandra: Well, it's quite nice.

Scout: What do you do?

Sandra: Jesus Christ.

Scout: I know what happens – I'm not stupid, you know. I mean what do you *do*?

Sandra: This is ridiculous. You're my brother.

Scout: So?

Sandra: Well, you're supposed to be a bit more self-conscious about these things.

Scout: I am self conscious – that's why I'm asking you.

Sandra: You just screw.

Scout: But how do you start?

Sandra: I don't know … you just start kissing.

Scout: But where were you?

Sandra: What does it matter where we were?

Scout: I was just asking.

Sandra: We were round his house.

Scout: Alone?

Sandra: Of course we were alone. We weren't going to do it with his mam there. Look, why don't you get yourself a girlfriend and find out for yourself?

Scout: I don't particularly want a girlfriend.

Sandra: Well, you don't need to know then.

Scout: Just because I don't want a girlfriend doesn't mean I shouldn't know about it.

Sandra: Well, you start kissing.

Scout: And?

Sandra: Then he starts feeling you up.

Scout: You mean touching your fanny?

Sandra: If you want to be crude about it.

Scout: I'm not trying to be crude. I'm just trying to get the proper idea.

Sandra: And then I touch him up. And then we take off our pants and that.

Scout: Just like that?

Sandra: Well, after a while.

Scout: How long?

Sandra: I don't know. It depends.

Scout: And then you just do it?

Sandra: You touch each other first.

Scout: What, without any clothes on?

Sandra: It's not just about screwing, you know. That's why they
call it making love.

Scout: Were you in love, like?

(Pause)

Sandra: I don't think so.

Scout: So it was just having sex, then?

Sandra: I was just testing it out.

Scout: So what did you reckon?

Sandra: It was good. It was alright.

Scout: How long did it last?

Sandra: I don't know. About five minutes.

Scout: From start to finish?

Sandra: Maybe a bit longer.

Scout: Then what do you do?

Sandra: I had a fag.

Scout: You know only idiots smoke.

Sandra: For God's sake shut up.

Scout: And then that's it? You're done?

Sandra: Well, sometimes you can kiss a bit more, but that's it, basically.

Scout: Wow. *(Pause)* So what did it feel like?

Sandra: I told you.

Scout: No you didn't.

Sandra: It's … you know … fine. It's good.

Scout: Was it messy?

Sandra: Not that messy. Look, once you get good at it, it's supposed
to be amazing.

Scout: You mean you have to practice?

Sandra: You have orgasms. I can't be expected to get them yet.

Scout: Why not?

Sandra: They're notoriously difficult.

Scout: Are they?

Sandra: Plus, I've been doing it with complete dorks.

Scout: I thought you said you loved them.

Sandra: I said I wasn't sure.

Scout: Have you done it a lot then?

Sandra: A few times.

Scout: With different ones?

Sandra: I'm not going to keep doing it with the same one all the time, am I?

Scout: Why not?

Sandra: I don't want to go out with them. I just want to get pregnant.

Scout: So it wasn't an accident?

Sandra: Of course it wasn't an accident.

Scout: No wonder Mam went mental. *(Pause)* What do you think she'll do then?

Sandra: What can she do?

(Pause)

Scout: So does it feel good being pregnant?

Sandra: It's alright.

Scout: Alright?

Sandra: You're supposed to feel sick but it hasn't been that bad.

Scout: Don't you eat coal and anchovies and stuff?

Sandra: Don't believe everything people tell you. Especially about food.

Scout: You're not very fat.

Sandra: You don't get fat till later.

Scout: Oh.

Sandra: But can't you tell a bit?

Scout: No.

Sandra: Come here.

Scout: What?

Sandra: Feel.

Scout: No.

Sandra: There. Can you feel anything?

Scout: Your belly.

Sandra: What's it like?

Scout: Soft.
Sandra: But can you feel anything?
   (Pause)
Scout: No.
Sandra: Do you like uz?
Scout: What do you mean?
Sandra: Do you like uz?
Scout: When you're not being horrible.
Sandra: I'm not being horrible now, am I?
Scout: I don't know.
Sandra: Why did you ask uz all those questions?
Scout: What questions?
Sandra: About sex and that.
Scout: To find out.
Sandra: What? *(Pause)* You don't fancy uz do you?
Scout: No.
Sandra: Just as well.
Scout: Just as well what?
Sandra: It'd be unnatural.
Scout: Of course it would.

   MUSIC: *'I'm Livin' in Shame' – Diana Ross and The Supremes*

Sandra's Bedroom

Sandra: *(Reading)* There are a number of sexually transmitted
   diseases which can effect your pregnancy. Herpes: can cause
   pain, nausea and painful lesions. Herpes can be passed to
   a child as the mother gives birth. It is important that you not
   exacerbate your lesions: try wearing loose-fitting cotton
   underwear and dust them with cornflower. Gonorrhoea: can
   cause blindness, conjunctivitis and generalised infections in
   the foetus. Syphilis: foetal bone or tooth deformities, still births
   and brain damage. AIDS.
   (The sound of Sandra closing her book.)

   MUSIC: *'I'm Livin' in Shame' – Diana Ross and The Supremes*

Mam's Bedroom

Mam: (To Dad) Sometimes Alan, to be quite honest, I think I'm just hanging on by my fingernails and, you know, by the very tips of my fingers, and I'm slipping, and I don't know why I'm falling, I don't even know why I'm here at all ... like a dead weight, and all I can think of is, why? Why did she run? Why didn't you look? Why does she argue in the first place? Why the anger, Alan? Why the hatred? Why the baby? Why are you dead, Alan? ... Why are you dead? I don't know, maybe there isn't an answer, maybe this is all there is ... this is living.

Kitchen

Mam: What do you think I should do?

Scout: I don't know. I don't know what the options are.

Mam: Stephen, there aren't any options.

Scout: Are there not?

Mam: You don't seriously think she can have this baby, do you?

Scout: Well, there was that programme on Oprah.

Mam: That was telling you not to have babies.

Scout: But wouldn't it be fun to have a baby brother?

Mam: I can't believe you're saying this, Stephen. I thought you had more sense. Of course it would not be fun to have a baby brother. It's not like a Christmas present.

Scout: Unless you're Jesus.

Mam: What do you mean by that?

Scout: Well, Jesus was a Christmas present for Mary.

Mam: I don't see what that's got to do it.

Scout: It was a joke.

Mam: Well, it wasn't funny – it's not fair on you, for a start.

Scout: I don't mind.

Mam: You might say that now but you don't know what it's like to have a baby.

Scout: What is it like, like?

Mam: It's a lot of hard work.

Scout: I don't mind.

Mam: That's not the point.

Scout: I like hard work.

Mam: The point is it will ruin her life.

(Long pause)

Scout: Isn't it ruined already?

Mam: Of course it isn't ruined already. What on earth made you say that?

Scout: You know, with Dad dying.

(Pause)

Mam: We'll get over that. We'll all get over it.

Scout: When?

(Pause)

Mam: I don't know. We have to be patient.

Scout: Do you believe it's possible to bring people back to life?

Mam: No.

Scout: Are you sure?

Mam: I'm positive.

Scout: So that could never happen to Dad? Not even in Africa?

Mam: Not anywhere.

Scout: But ... Mam there must be something. You know I do everything, I try my best all the time, I do everything to make it right for Sandra and you, I don't mean to make things bad ... I don't mean to cause trouble and that, Mam. I just want to stop feeling lonely, I hate feeling alone.

Mam: You're doing ever so well, Stephen. Please, just be strong for me.

Scout: OK. I'll try.

MUSIC: *'Reflections' – Diana Ross and The Supremes*

Sandra's Bedroom

Sandra: *(Reading)* Flatulence: this is quite a common problem
during the first few months of pregnancy. The change of diet,
internal pressure on the digestive tract, emotional and physical
changes in your body, can all contribute to flatulence, this is
nothing to be embarrassed about. Fortunately this unpleasant
irritation can cause no long term damage to either you or your
foetus. Remember don't gulp, don't gorge and steer clear of
Brussels sprouts, fried foods and baked beans.

MUSIC: *Introduction to 'Reflections' – Diana Ross
and The Supremes*

Mam's Bedroom

Sandra: What are you doing?
Scout: Shhh. Keep your voice down.
Sandra: What's going on?
Scout: Shut the door. *(Sandra shuts the door.)* I'm looking for
something.
Sandra: What?
Scout: Shoes.
Sandra: In Mam's cupboard?
Scout: Not Mam's shoes. Dad's.
Sandra: They'll never fit you.
Scout: I don't want to wear them.
Sandra: Why not?
Scout: I'm going to bury them.
Sandra: Bury them?
Scout: Yes.
   (Scout rummages in the cupboard.)
Sandra: Are you out of your head?
Scout: Shit. I don't know where she's put them.
Sandra: I think she threw them out.
Scout: What did she do that for?

Sandra: I don't know.

(Scout goes on rummaging.)

Scout: Stupid cow.

Sandra: Just calm down.

Scout: She must have kept one pair.

Sandra: Remember – she gave them to Oxfam.

Scout: What? She's sent them to the third world?

Sandra: They sell them, stupid. In Gosforth.

Scout: It's ridiculous. There's nothing here. Not even shirts or anything.

Sandra: I felt something.

Scout: What?

Sandra: Something move.

Scout: You're not going to have it now, are you?

Sandra: Don't be stupid, it was just kicking.

Scout: And you could feel it?

Sandra: Of course.

Scout: It can't be very big.

Sandra: It can still kick.

Scout: Can I feel?

Sandra: Go on.

Scout: There's nothing there.

Sandra: It must have stopped.

Scout: I'd thought you'd be fatter than that.

Sandra: Fatter than what?

Scout: To have it kicking and everything.

Sandra: You get fatter towards the end.

Scout: Are you really going to have it?

Sandra: Course.

Scout: Even after what Mam said?

Sandra: She has to let uz. She's taking uz to the doctor's.

Scout: Do you really think it's wise?

Sandra: I thought you wanted me to have it.

Scout: I do. I just never thought it would cause so many problems. *(Violent rummaging)* This stuff's shit.

Sandra: What's the matter with you?

Scout: There's nothing here.

Sandra: I don't know why you want to bury a shoe in the first place.

Scout: Well, why do you want a baby?

Sandra: If it's that important you can have one of mine.

Scout: I don't want one of yours.

Sandra: But not them new black ones.

Scout: I want to bury the shoe because then you can bring a person back to life.

(Pause)

Sandra: Stephen!

Scout: It's ridiculous.

(Sounds of Scout throwing things across the room.)

Sandra: Calm down.

Scout: Shut up, you.

Sandra: You're the one being ridiculous.

Scout: It's not ridiculous. Not necessarily.

Sandra: I think you need to get a grip on things.

Scout: Me?

Mam: *(Downstairs)* Stephen? *(Pause)* Sandra?

(Mam comes up the stairs.)

Sandra: Yes, you.

(The door opens.)

Mam: What on earth's going on in here?

(Pause)

Sandra: Nothing.

Mam: Have you farted?

MUSIC: *'Wishin' and Hopin' ' – Dusty Springfield*

Living Room

Mam: *(On the phone)* The problem is Mam ... all I'm saying ...
Mam, will you please ... ju... Mam, listen ... just ... Mam
... please listen to me ... Look, all I'm saying is ... you can't ...
you can't just pin somebody down and give them an abortion,
Mam. Listen, Mam! Mam, stop shouting! Mam ... you have
to let people make their own minds up ... Mam ... Mam ...
I can't cope with this ... Mam, I've gotta go. *(She puts the phone
down. Pause)* Sandra – were you listening to me?

Sandra: No.

Mam: You were, weren't you? You've been behind there all this
time listening.

Sandra: I wasn't anywhere.

Mam: Well, of course you were somewhere.

Sandra: No I wasn't.

Mam: Don't be perverse.

Sandra: I'm perverted am I? 'Cos I was behind the door? Because
I wanna bring life into the world?

Mam: Oh, Sandra love ...

Sandra: Don't oh Sandra me.

Mam: That's not what I meant. I didn't know you were there.

Sandra: Well, why did you say it?

Mam: Because you were getting at me. Insistently.

Sandra: I'm not getting at anyone. You're just closed down.

Mam: Sandra, you're the one whose closed down, you're not
listening to anything anyone says.

Sandra: I'm listening to everything.

Mam: Look, please let's not get into another fight.

Sandra: It's not a fight, it's a discussion.

Mam: Please.

Sandra: You're just jealous.

Mam: Jealous? Of what?

Sandra: I'm not stupid

Mam: Why would I be jealous, Sandra? I'm not jealous.

Sandra: I know, Mam.

Mam: I have no idea what you are on about.
Sandra: That you wouldn't screw him.
   (Pause)
Mam: Screw him?
Sandra: Dad. I'm not stupid.
Mam: That's none of your business.
Sandra: It is now.
Mam: You're too young to understand.
Sandra: Yawn, yawn.
Mam: Why are you doing this to me?
Sandra: Just because you don't like it, doesn't mean other
   people don't.
Mam: Stop it.
Sandra: You know what I like Mam? I like it when people lick uz
   all over. What turns you on?
Mam: We are not going to talk about this.
Sandra: Oral sex.
Mam: Sandra. I'm not listening to this.
Sandra: Or a pearl necklace. Do you know what that is?
Mam: What do you want for dinner?
   (They start to speak over one another.)
Sandra: And in the shower. Have you ever done it in the shower?
Mam: What do you want?
Sandra: Eh?
Mam: I'm not listening. I could make some pasta.
Sandra: Then one time …
Mam: I think there's some pesto left.
Sandra: Listen to me …
   (Their conversation reaches a crescendo.)
Mam: *(Shouting)* Shut up! Shut up! *(Silence. A pause.)* Just answer
   me, Sandra. What do you want for your dinner?
Sandra: Sausages.

MUSIC: *Introduction to 'Someday We'll Be Together' – Diana Ross
and The Supremes*

Scout's Bedroom

Scout: *(Reading)* Dear Dad, I know you can't hear this probably, but I am saying it just in case. I mean, I've got nothing to lose, have I? I mean, not considering. We've all missed you since you've been gone. I am still in the Scouts. Mam sent us to Grandma's but we're back home now. I think Mam's a bit depressed and Sandra's pregnant. She's going to have a baby and name it after you. Dad, sometimes I think of this and I'm scared for Sandra. I read in a book that having a baby's quite difficult and everything and even though it would be cush to have a baby and everything and Sandra let me feel her tummy, I don't want for anyone to come to any harm. Actually, I could hardly feel anything. Mam and Sandra have been arguing nearly every day 'cos Mam thinks that Sandra is too young and should do her G C S E s, but by the time Sandra actually has the baby she will be in the fifth year and then it will be nearly legal. So if you are in heaven and can have a word with God or anything then can you please tell him to make them stop fighting and that. I have got a new friend now, Jimmy Spud. We are going to do a thing to bring you back to life. But I don't want to get your hopes up. Anyway, if you know where any of your shoes are, please try and tell uz somehow. Maybe you can give uz a sign. I'd better go now. Your loving son, Stephen.

M U S I C : *'Someday We'll Be Together'* – *Diana Ross and The Supremes*

Mam's Bedroom

Sandra: Mam.
Mam: What is it?
Sandra: Can I come in?
Mam: It's very late, Sandra.
Sandra: I need to talk to you.
Mam: I'll just switch the light on.
(The sound of the light going on.)

Mam: Are you all right, Sandra?

(Pause)

Sandra: Mam, you must think I'm a right bitch.

(Pause)

Mam: No I don't. I'm just trying very hard to understand what's happening.

Sandra: I just wanted to say I'm sorry. For what I said the other day.

Mam: I see.

Sandra: About oral sex and that.

Mam: Please Sandra, you don't have to go into details.

Sandra: I mean, it probably wasn't the best of times to go into it.

Mam: No.

Sandra: And after all, you are my mother.

Mam: I'm sorry too.

Sandra: What for?

Mam: For the things I said.

Sandra: That I was perverted?

Mam: You know I didn't mean it like that. *(Pause)* I'm just terrified in case something happens to you. It's so easy for things to go wrong. I mean, one minute you're riding along fine, not a care in the world, and the next … *(Pause)* When you've been through all the things that I've been through, you start to see how important it is not to have problems, not to have to worry about the bills. I lie awake at night and I just don't think we'll be able to manage. You know, I just want you to have a break in life.

Sandra: I thought we were rich.

Mam: We're not rich. I'm going to have to start looking for a job.

Sandra: What you gonna do?

Mam: I don't know. *(Pause)* I know this is a cliché, but when I was your age I had this idea, well these images in my mind, of what would happen. You know, I wanted to be an artist or something and live in a big house in the country. You have all these idealistic visions of how things are. And it's never very easy. I mean, it's not that things have gone badly. Dad had a good job. And there's you and Stephen, but …

Sandra: But?

Mam: None of it's been particularly easy.

Sandra: Are you trying to tell uz I'm being idealistic?

Mam: I was just thinking out loud. *(Pause)* I feel as if I've been kicked all over this year.

Sandra: Mam, I know that I've been bad, that I've done stupid things and that, well, since Dad died I've been, you know, difficult. And that you think I've been irresponsible and childish and that this is some kind of attention seeking or some cry for help or something. But it isn't like that. I don't sit and think of the future and think things will be great, but I thought of what I want now. For the next few years anyway. You don't know how carefully I've looked into things. And I need something tangible, Mam. I suppose in a way I need something to replace Dad. Some sort of life, so there's a point. And it's not bringing him back, or grieving or anything. It's much deeper. Why shouldn't I feel like this? Why shouldn't I wanna have a child? Mam, people go through their whole lives without feeling settled. Do you understand what I'm saying? Do you understand?

Mam: It just seems so drastic. A few years would make all the difference.

Sandra: See – that's exactly what I'm talking about.

Mam: I'm just trying to explain.

Sandra: I know this is not what you expected. But you never expected Dad to get run over. You never expected Grandma to marry that man. You never expected Stephen to be a Scout. Mam, nearly everything's unexpected.

Mam: Lover.

Sandra: I'm just trying to tell you. I'm not doing this out of hate. I'm doing it out of love.

Mam: I just feel exhausted.

Sandra: Sometimes you just have to accept things.

Mam: I think you should go back to bed now.

Sandra: Do you understand what I'm saying though?

Mam: Let's discuss it all tomorrow.
Sandra: Mam, do you still love uz?
Mam: Of course I do.
Sandra: Do you mean that?
Mam: Of course.

MUSIC: *'Will You Love Me Tomorrow?'* – *The Shirelles*

Sandra's Bedroom

(The sound of tapping on the window.)

Sandra: Ah!
Scout: *(Outside)* Sandra!
Sandra: Who is it?
Scout: *(Outside)* It's me.
Sandra: What the hell are you doing out there?
Scout: *(Outside)* Let uz in.
Sandra: Jesus Christ!
    (Sandra starts to open the window.)
Scout: *(Outside)* Hurry up. It's freezing.
Sandra: What the hell are doing out there in your pyjamas.
Scout: The door just locked. I couldn't get in.
Sandra: But it's three o' clock in the morning.
Scout: I know.
Sandra: And what the hell's that?
Scout: It's a trowel.
Sandra: What do you want a trowel for?
Scout: I needed it to dig the hole.
Sandra: What hole?
Scout: For the sock.
Sandra: What sock?
Scout: I couldn't find a shoe.
Sandra: What shoe?
Scout: To bring back Dad.
Sandra: Jesus Christ! Are you out of your head?

Scout: It was hopeless. We were just burying it and then we were interrupted.

Sandra: Who was burying it?

Scout: Jimmy Spud. Then his Mam came.

Sandra: I'm not surprised. You're freezing.

Scout: I know.

Sandra: Look, I think you're going to have to stop this.

Scout: But it's to bring him back.

Sandra: Nothing can bring him back. You just have to accept it.

Scout: Why should I accept it?.

Sandra: Because trying to bring him back won't do you any good.

Scout: Well, what good are you doing?

Sandra: I'm not doing any good I'm just trying to get on with things. Stephen, the universe is just a load of atoms and sometimes they come together and then they are certain things and then they stop being in that combination and they are something else. It's just physics.

Scout: It's not just physics.

Sandra: There's no point in being annoyed.

Scout: But there must be something else.

Sandra: Why are you getting so angry?

Scout: Because I hate it. I hate you. I hate everything.

Sandra: There's nothing to hate. You're just annoyed because you feel helpless. Look, everyone feels helpless. But if Dad was here he'd want you to stop thinking about the past and start doing things that you can make a difference over.

Scout: What sort of things?

Sandra: I don't know. Stuff at Scouts or something.

Scout: Well, what are you doing?

Sandra: I'm having a baby. At least it'll be mine. Someone I can look after and everything.

Scout: But what can I do? I can't have a baby can I? All I can do is this. It doesn't make any sense. Why did he have to die? Why are you having a stupid baby? Why is Mam so weird? I just want it to stop, So it all goes back to what it was before. Remember before when everything was OK. At nights and that I listen

to Mam's door and everything and she's crying, 'cos you've
been shouting at her. And I know I want to have a nephew and
everything but I don't want it to make everything horrible.
I want it to make things better, and all it does is make it worse.
So why shouldn't I plant a few stupid socks, it doesn't make
any difference anyway. And you never know.
(Pause)
Sandra: I'm sorry, Stephen. I didn't mean to make this hard for
you. But it wouldn't be like this if she wasn't such a lunatic.
Scout: But Dad's just died. What do you expect? *(Pause)* Maybe
you just want to have a baby as sort of compensation.
Sandra: What?
Scout: Because it'll help you come to terms with things.
Sandra: Who are you – the Brain of Britain?
Scout: Well, I'm just saying.
Sandra: Of course I want to have it as compensation. But every-
thing you do is some sort of compensation. It's compensation
for being born, for being alive, for living in this stupid house.
Scout: Don't you like living here?
Sandra: Of course I don't. I hate it. Do you?
Scout: I thought we were starting to get along.
Sandra: Well …
Scout: Sandra, will you give me a cuddle?
Sandra: Me?
Scout: Please.
Sandra: Why?
Scout: I feel lonely.
   (They cuddle.)
Scout: Do you think it'll all work out?
Sandra: I hope so.
Scout: Thanks. For the cuddle.
Sandra: Where are you going?
Scout: I've decided I might as well finish it.
Sandra: What?
Scout: The burying. Can you help me out of this window?

The Garden

Scout: Dad, I've been trying really hard recently … I've done everything I can think of. If this doesn't work then I'm giving up, it's just too hard … Every night I listen to the wall and hear Mam … sometimes I listen with Sandra. You've got to do something Dad, please.

The Kitchen

Sandra: Mam.
Mam: Sandra.
Sandra: Are you crying?
Mam: *(Sobbing)* Yes
Sandra: Please don't. Not in the kitchen.
Mam: I can't stop myself.
Sandra: Come here. Hold me.
   (Sounds of cuddling.)
Mam: I'm scared, sweetheart.
Sandra: It'll be alright.
Mam: I think about everything.
Sandra: I know.
Mam: It doesn't make any sense.
Sandra: I think you're overwhelmed.
Mam: I just don't know what to say anymore
Sandra: Mam, you've said everything. That's what Mams do.
Mam: I'm sorry, lover
Sandra: That's alright.

Sandra's Bedroom

Scout: *(Reading)* Your first visit to the Doctor. The Doctor will give you a thorough physical examination and will enquire about your family history. Remember the Doctor's not there to judge you, he is your friend for what is after all the beginning of the most exciting, rewarding and fulfilling experience of your life.

   MUSIC: *'Baby Love' – Diana Ross and The Supremes*

Outside the Doctor's Surgery

(Long pause)

Mam: I can't believe it.

Sandra: I think we should go to someone else.

Mam: Sandra, you're not pregnant.

Sandra: Of course I am.

Mam: Sandra, she said so. Categorically.

Sandra: But I must be.

Mam: Sandra, you haven't even had sex.

(Pause)

Sandra: I must have had.

(Pause)

Mam: Look, it's alright. I'm sorry. *(Pause)* Just thank God.

Sandra: All I wanted was a little boy.

Mam: I know.

Sandra: You're glad aren't you?

Mam: *(Pause)* I'm relieved, Sandra.

Sandra: We have to go somewhere else.

Mam: I had no idea – we'll go home and sleep on this. Maybe we can get some help.

Sandra: Help?

Mam: OK?

Sandra: You think I'm deluded or something. That I'm mental. You're the one who's deluded. At least I tried to get what I want, Mam. At least I tried to make things better.

Mam: Sandra, I think you're still in shock.

Sandra: You're gloating.

Mam: I just think you've been through quite a lot.

Sandra: I haven't been through anything.

(Pause)

Mam: We'll patch everything. It'll be all right. *(Pause)* Just remember, through all of this, I never stopped loving you. *(Long pause – she is not so sure)* Really.

Sandra: Well. After all, there's always next time.

MUSIC: *'Baby Love' – Diana Ross and The Supremes*

Sandra's Bedroom

Sandra: *(Reading)* Coping with loss. Whatever the cause of your loss, the world will seem as if it's crashing down on you. You've felt its heartbeat, you've chosen its cot, told your friends, knitted sweaters – there is probably no greater loss than losing a child. You must take steps to lessen the inevitable depression.

See your baby, hold your baby, name your child. You can't grieve a child that has no name, or a child that you have never seen. This will make the death more real to you. Ask not to be sedated. Cry – for as long as you like, for as much as you need to. This is a natural part of the grieving process and nothing to be embarrassed about.

You will ask yourself 'Why?', but this philosophical question cannot be answered. You may look upon it as God's will or as a random sequence of events over which we have no control. Death is the great imponderable, something we can do nothing to avoid and nothing to alter. The more we accept our powerlessness, the more empowered we become.

Doorway to the House

(The sound of the door opening.)

Mam: In you go.
Sandra: I'm going upstairs.
Scout: Mam! Mam!
(Mam hurries in to find Scout.)

The Living Room

Scout: Look who's here!
Mam: Alan!

MUSIC: *'My Boyfriend's Back' – The Angels*

THE END

Part 4 of GOD'S COUNTRY

Spoonface Steinberg

Character

SPOONFACE STEINBERG   A girl

The music in the play is taken from
Callas: La Divina 1 and 2 (EMI Classics)

Spoonface Steinberg was first performed on Radio 4
on 27 January 1997 with the following cast:

SPOONFACE STEINBERG   Becky Simpson

Director   Kate Rowland

MUSIC: *Maria Callas singing 'Casta Diva' from* Norma *by Bellini*

(Spoonface talks over the music)

Spoonface: In the olden days – when they wrote the songs and the operas and that, it mattered how you died – when the singers singed and went about – and they sang like beautiful birds and they fell over and everything – and she was all quavery and beautiful and everyone holded their breath – and there she was in the special light with her boobs and everything – and everyone would be looking and they would cry and in their hearts they would weep for the poor lady – the poor poor lady who dies so well.

And if I could ever grow up I would be one of them sad singers and do the dying and everybody would clap and cheer – and in all of the singing when people heard it they would have a little piece of beauty – which is very important – to have the little piece of beauty what's in the music – and this is what I realised – even though the beautiful singing is sad – it is still happy in a way – the saddest things fill you up – like in a big way and you feel so full as in no happiness can bring such – and all such sadness is beautiful – as beautiful as the singing – as beautiful as the dying – and it would make a meaning – and I would sing the dying and people would love me – and I would sing the dying and out come the angels to take me away – and I would sing the dying and there would be a lovely piece of beauty in the world – and I would sing the dying and be as free as a little bird floating up to heaven.

MUSIC: *Maria Callas singing 'Casta Diva' from* Norma

I never heard such singing before except for when Doctor Bernstein brought the tapes – even though the other children like such music as Take That and that – even one little girl has this tape of Take That and Take That sent her this picture and they were all blowing her a kiss and all she ever does is play the music and she can't even hear because she is in a coma and then Take That made her a tape which said 'Hello this is Robbie' and she still wasn't better – and I said this was no surprise on account of the tape – but I play the proper music – it is so sad – and it is about the dying and it makes me so clear.

I was never right ever since I was born – this means that I do very bad writing and that I can't speak proper and that I am backwards and that I am a special child – but why is a mystery for what they have not got an answer – but Mam said when I was born it was at a dark night and it was raining and thundery and all the cats and dogs and things were under the tables – and the wind was screeching round everywhere – and everything was quite horrible – but I didn't mind because I was just little and I was in the hospital and Mam kissed me and when she looked at my face she noticed that it was round – and everyone came and looked at my face – and they laughed and said I was Spoonface because when they looked at my face it was round as a spoon and when you look into a spoon you see this face just like mine – and that is how I came to be Spoonface Steinberg – because my other name is Steinberg – but I never even knew because I was just a little baby and all the stars and planets were moving inside of me and I was looking up and the world was as bright as colours and as shimmery as light and I was just a baby – and when you're a baby you have a soft head and that – and that's what makes you backwards. Sometimes when it's very late at night – when they think I'm asleep, Mam says to Dad that maybe it is his fault that I am not right – on the fact that on the day Dad came back when he was out with the floozie, I did fall off the chair – Dad came back and it was quite late for our tea and I was sitting on the chair and Mam said that Dad was out with someone – and Dad says he was in the office doing the meeting – and Mam said she phoned the meeting and he was off with the office doing a floozie – and that this was one of his students – and she was going somewhere – off with the final straw – then there was all this crying and screaming and Dad went

like a beetroot and Mam said that the student was just a baby and
had big boobs and I fell over – it was like when you bump your
head only worse – and then everything went white like lighten-
ing – and this was bad on account of my softness – and they were
crying there with me and I was silent as a worm – and Dad told
Mam he would not ever have another floozie if Mam would be
nicer and Mam said she would be nicer – and then it was that
everything was alright – except I started going backwards – but
I am not sure if this is to do with it or not – maybe it is – maybe
it is not – I think I was backwards before the fall – before Dad came
back and everything – I think I was always backwards ever since
I was born and there was all the thunder and that, and I think ever
since I was born that my brain was quite special – I think I have
a special brain what is quite different in how it was and stuff – but
nobody knows for sure – all the experts with all their computers
and all the doctors who poke in your ear and look into your brain
and all the people who do the quizzes and all questioners and such
like – none of them know for certain – they all said no one can
know can ever know for certain – and that's what Dad says – he
says there is only one thing for certain – nobody knows anything
for certain – what is true I think – on account that he is a lecturer
of philosophy – the thing is even now I am old I cannot read
proper or to write and am very bad at games and that I cannot go
to a proper school as I am not allowed on account of my brain –
but I am quite a special little girl, though – that's what Mrs Spud
says – Mrs Spud does the cleaning – and she says that I am
quite one of the special girls she has ever known and every time
she comes she brings me a sweetie which is very nice for she has so
many problems of her own – she says that everybody is different
and that it is quite good indeed and that we should all be happy
and that – for every person is a very special person and that it is
good to be different as if there's no difference we would all be the
same – and Mrs Spud told me not to worry about my brain because
to be different is to be who you are – so I do not believe that
I fell on my head – I do not believe that I was affected – or
it was Dad's fault for the floozie or Mam's fault 'cos I was

unattended – I believe that I was supposed to be backward –
I believe it was all part of what is supposed to be – and when
I was born God came and touched me on my head – down he
came and touched my soft spot and made me me.

MUSIC: *Maria Callas singing 'Mon cœur s'ouvre à ta voix'
from* Samson et Dalila *by Saint-Saëns*

One day I started to do the numbers. This was when Dad came
back from the university and he was with a calculator for doing
the marks. He was sat doing the marks when he said two numbers
and I went 42 – because it was the answer of the two numbers –
and then he goes – goodness me – and then he said two more
numbers and I said 147 – which was another answer – and then he
did more and more – and some of the answers he had to do on
the calculator – and then he started shouting of Mam – and Mam
came running as if there was something bad – but it was only me
doing the numbers and I did more and more – and Mam kissed
me and was crying and that – and Dad kept doing more and more
and he was laughing – and Mam said he had to stop – and I said
what was it that had made her cry? – and she said that it was
because of the numbers and never in the world did they know
I could do the numbers – but I could do them now – and I was a
genius – and it was of my brain.

And then I had to do them in front of a doctor – and then
the doctor said – if Spoonface can do numbers then she can do
dates – and then I did some – this is how I do it – what is the day of
July the 4th 2010? – Saturday – amazing, absolutely amazing – and
that is how I do the dates and they have to look it up in a book
as soon as I've said the answer and there it is – and they say how
do I know so many numbers? and I say I don't know – and how do
I know so many dates? – and I also say I don't know – but it's just
obvious like colours – and that is why – and Mrs Spud says that is
why we are all different – to me the numbers are obvious and to
her some other stuff is obvious – like how to clean the loo and
that – but at least that means we're all different.

So this is all because I am autistic — and that is quite a big strain on Mam and Dad which was account of why they did split up — for a start Mam was quite sad — she was in the house when Dad went to work and she did look at her books and such like as she was getting a Ph.D. also like Dad — only he finished quicker on account of women have to have babies that men can't have — this meant that her's was much slower — and she would sit in the room and when ever she was just to do some work I came in and then she had to stop — and it wasn't fair of me to do the Ph.D. — and Dad was on the committees — so Mam had to drink the vodka — and she used to sit with the book and the vodka — and Dad came back and she said — that he was not of attention — and maybe he wasn't.

Then one day Dad said he had met one person who was doing a different Ph.D. to Mam and that she was very nice and that he would go away to live with her for a bit — and Mam said she was glad of him to go — and even though I was backwards and that — it would be better than his stupid face — and off Dad went for a bit until sometimes he came back for a few minutes on a Saturday.

Then Mam used to have more and more — and she would come to me and say 'My poor sweet angel, my poor sweet angel' — and then drink the vodka — and then she had to take tablets off the Doctor and would stop the vodka at the same time — except one time she had the pills and the vodka and went to sleep on the stair and I put on her a nice blanket in case anyone tripped — but nobody did trip as there was only me — then the next day Mrs Spud came and tidied up where she had been sick.

MUSIC: *Maria Callas singing 'Teneste la promessa'
from* La Traviata *by Verdi*

When I first started feeling funny that is when I still had hair — it was hardly noticeable at first — that was there was hardly nothing wrong except I was tired a bit — but then Mam was very worried that I was thinner and thinner and one day I might fade away to

a speck – and that I was looking peaky – but because I'm backwards then I wasn't very good at saying what is wrong – so she took
me straight to the doctor in case I disappeared – and the doctor
looked at me like this ... and he said – 'Oh deary me, Spoonface
will have to go straight to the hospital' – which is where I went – it
was alright as I had been before to do the numbers – they were all
very nice to me and the doctors held onto my hand and stuff and
they all smiled which means something is wrong – and then Mam
looked greyish and they said they were going to have to put me in a
tube, which was quite horrible as I am only little – I did not wish
to go into the tube but they said I would have to on account of
being so thin – and inside the tube they would find out what it
was – so I went in the tube and Mam was watching when I went
in and waved bye bye – and then all these computers went off and
stuff – and they did all this dialling and whirring and then there was
some rays or something – and I was in there like it was a space
machine but it never went anywhere except in the hospital even
though it took ages – and I waited and all the computers were
doing different numbers and all the information was going everywhere and that – and then it came time for me to come out and
when I came out there was Mam and the doctor waiting and they
said hello and I was allowed out – the doctor said he would have
to check the switches and that we should all go into a room where
Mam could cry and I could play with Lego – when I was in the
room I got a drink of pop and Mam said it was unexpected that
we would go straight to the hospital and go into a tube – then
the doctor came back and said that he had got an answer off the
machines and the answer was – that I was going to die.

MUSIC: *Maria Callas singing 'Addio, del passato'*
from La Traviata *by Verdi*

Mam looked very sad and said the doctors must have wonky
computers and that they needed to put me in the tube again – but
then they said how the computers were only new and that they
were very expensive and that it was definite what they said – and it

was that I was still going to die – only they said there was hope –
that there was always hope – and anyway, it would take a long time
for me to die so we went home for some tea – when we went
home in the car there was rain and wind and everything and we
passed this accident where a man on a motorbike had got his head
smashed off – and Mam said that even if I was supposed to die there
would still be hope 'cos there was millions of people that were
saved by God everyday – even if the poor man was smashed on the
road – and so it was better not be too worried about it – so I said
I wasn't worried and we had fish fingers.

Then Mam had to phone Dad – he was with the granduate – in
a little flat and everything – and Mam rang and the granduate
answered and said that she would still like to meet Mam as there
was no hard feelings but Mam said she had to speak to Dad quick –
normally she used to shout at him saying, 'What did I do? What
did I do?' – but this time she said to the granduate to get right off as
she needed to talk to Dad immediately – then on came Dad and
Mam said there was something terrible wrong with Spoonface
and that she'd been in a tube and had been playing with the Lego
and they said she was going to die and he must come at once – and
then she put the phone down – and Dad came and said this was
the last thing he expected – especially as we had so many troubles
and he kissed me and he also kissed Mam and said – what such
troubles we had – first I wasn't born right, and that even though
I did numbers, I wasn't very good at games and stuff – and then he
went off with a graduand too young for him and stuff and Mam
was living here with only me – and now I was going to die.

Mam said she was sorry and that deep down she really loved
Dad, and Dad was sorry that he really loved Mam and they all loved
me over and over – I was supposed to be asleep by now but I could
hear them and of everything they said – it was so terrible for
everyone and this was the change of everything – and then they
came in at the door and looked at me in the dark where I was
supposed to be asleep – and I was lying in my beautiful bed with all

the covers up and they would stare like this at me ... and have
their arms holding each other and they whispered that I was a poor
little soul – but they never knew I was wide awake and I could
see them through the crack in my eye as not to scare them – and
when I looked at them and I saw that they were crying – and then
Dad said: there I was fast asleep not a care in the world – but this
was ridiculous because I was there awake all the time.

MUSIC: *Maria Callas singing 'Ebben? ne andrò lontana'*
from La Wally *by Catalani*

After a while Dad came back to see us quite a bit – some nights
he used to stay in Mam's bed and everything and he would see
me in the morning – and the Ph.D. said that she had a new boyfriend who was quite young and played in a musical group and that
Dad was quite old to be living at her house and Dad was to live
all alone except when he came to see us – and when he came he
was nicer than ever – and Mam was quite happy sometimes but she
would cry at night when I couldn't hear who she was – I kept
going to the hospital and they would do all these checks on me and
go, 'Oh well, it is very bad indeed' – Mam would be worried and
tell me to be brave – then one day they said, 'Spoonface is going to
die, except we might put her in this machine and she would get
some rays and stuff and then she would be better' – but I couldn't
go in straight away on account of the list so I waited a few days and
stuff – and Dad came round every night and that – and he said
that Mam was to go out to see her friend and he would stay and
watch me – but he never 'cos he was downstairs and he found
Mam's vodka – I was feeling quite sickly and I was all wobbly
because I was thin as a stick so I went straight to bed – then I was
asleep – then there was this noise and in came Dad and he smelt
really weird – and he came right up to my nose – like he has flying
over my nose which was horrible – and his eyes were sort of fat
and soft – and he had one of the glasses from downstairs and the
vodka what Mam kept in the freezer – and he took this huge gulp

and went pink – I just looked at him like this – wishing Mam was
back – then he grabbed my arm and it was quite hard – he did grab
me tight like this … and I looked up and was frightened of what
he would do – and then I thought I was going to faint of the
pressure – and he started rocking backwards like this – and then
he said I had suffered the worse out of anyone in the world and it
was all his fault – that he didn't know what he was doing – that
he was such a young man and he was just a poor philosophy man
because he couldn't think of what else to do – and that he loved
Mam even though when they had such a young baby as myself it
was before things were settled – but then he said that he loved me
and he didn't know what he was doing except for that he was sorry
for it all – and especially sorry for his whole life - but then I was
Spoonface from his own sperm and that I was the most loved child
in the whole world – and even if I never understood a word I was
still the most loved child in all the world – and he went like this
for ages – and all of a sudden he stopped doing his grip and fell
backwards and plopped onto the floor – I wanted to go to the loo,
but I didn't ask in case he tried to grab me again – and I saw he was
sitting back like this … on the floor and his face was bright red
and he sort of shook – he was shaking and he did these gasps like he
couldn't breathe – and no tears would come from his crying just
these shakes – then I heard the door and Mam came up the stairs in
her coat and she saw Dad on the floor doing the shaking and she
just left him and picked me out of bed and put me in between her
bosoms and she pressed me there for a long time and kissed the tip
of my head – after that she took me to her room – she said that
Dad was over-whelmed and that he was reading of Kierkegaard
which was too bad for him – and the next day I was in Mam's bed
and Dad was in mine.

    And she said that not to worry about Dad that he was very sorry
from gripping me so hard and it was all 'cos of the vodka – and
he promised he would never shake again.

MUSIC: *Maria Callas singing 'O mio babbino caro'*
from Gianni Schicchi *by Puccini*

I love the beautiful women who do the operas and how they
sing and they flutter their voices like this – because it is the saddest
things are the best things of all – and that is because God made all
the sad things for to make us human and this is what Doctor
Bernstein said at the hospital when I went in – he was quite old
and stuff and he said that I was very brave and I should be very
brave because when his Mam was little she was very brave as well
even though she was in a concentration camp.

Concentration camps were these places where they took Jewish
people to burn – this is what the doctor said – he said that there
were loads of people and they all had to sleep on one bunk and
that – and the Nazis shot them and then they starved them and it
was horrible for his poor Mam because she was just little – in the
whole history of the world there has never been anything as awful
as the concentration camps, but what happened to the poor people
there was to show that they never gave up hope – and that never
mind the worse thing that could happen to people they could not
stop them from being human beings – some of the little children
were skinnier than I am now with the cancer, and all that was
wrong with them was they didn't eat – just this soup what didn't
have any vegetables in it – and they'd just be standing there and
their Mammies and Daddies would be bashed – like there was one
little girl who was with her Mam and the soldier came and hit
her Mam on the head and shot her and then she died and the poor
little girl just had to stand there – that little girl was the Mam of
the doctor – and there were millions and millions of people like
this – so in comparison to me it is much worse – and I felt sorry for
the doctor when he told me these things as he had a little cry in
the corner of his eye – and he never said any of this to scare me –
he said all of this to help me because the whole lesson of the stories
was that little children were braver than everybody else *(underneath
her voice we hear Maria Callas singing 'Casta Diva' and then 'Mon cœur
s'ouvre à ta voix')* and all the little children all played games in the

middle of mud – in the middle of the concentration camp they
played – and this was the human spirit – in the middle where their
Mams and Dads was getting gassed – and they could kill their Mams
and stuff but they couldn't kill what was in the minds of the children –
this was the lesson – that no matter how bad it is for us while we
are dying it is still a wonderful thing that we are alive – this is what the
doctor said – and he said when the soldiers came and took the poor
little children to the ovens and the poor children and everything
thought they were going for a wash but everybody knew really that
they were going to get gassed – because they had seen the smoke of
burning bodies – then the children were waiting outside and all the
little children wrote things on the walls – on the walls of the gas cham-
ber where they were about to be cooked. And some little children
wrote poems – and some little children drew pictures – and even today
you can see the pictures of butterflies on the outside – little butterflies
that were flying up to God – beautiful butterflies with tender wings
that would brush their faces and kiss them better before they flew –
careful little butterflies in all the death and the mud and every
thing – and that day when he told me this I cried for the butterflies
and the little children – and all their sad faces drifting up to heaven.

And the doctor said that his Grandma used to be a singer of the
opera before she went to this place – and in them days everyone loved
the opera – not like now when everyone likes Take That – and when
they would put the lights out – all the poor women on the bunks
would think of their husbands who were never to be seen – and they
would ask Grandma Bernstein to sing – and in the sad dark she would
sing – sing to all the poor skinny women – and she sang all the songs
what she knew in the opera – and she sang for the poor people in
the bunks – and all the poor people who had died – and she sang for
the children of the people to come – and that was very important
to everyone to have such songs to be sung – and then I would play
the music and in the heart of it I could hear the singing of the poor
Grandma on her bunk – and the poor children who wrote their
pictures on the wall – and even in the darkest place there was someone with such a beautiful song to sing.

MUSIC: *Maria Callas singing 'O mio babbino caro'*
from Gianni Schicchi

By the time I had to go into the machine I was quite upset that
I was going to die but then Mam told me not to be because it
would zap me and then I would be alright – but I knew that maybe
there was a chance that I would not be zapped proper – but I never
said anything – so I went in and got zapped – I went in every
day for three weeks they said that was quite enough as they didn't
want to zap too much as they might do a mischief – they gave me
centigrays – these are special rays which get the cancer and make it
better – they put me in the machine and then zapped the centi-
grays straight into me – and I felt so small as if I was travelling all
through the history of time to another place where all the things
were different – and in this place then everybody was laughing and
happy and there was no more hospitals or concentration camps
and everybody had ice cream and watched the telly and there was
opera people and everything – and all of a sudden I believed that
maybe I had died in the zapper and when I looked around that I
was in heaven – but then I came out and I had not died at all and
I was still in the hospital and there was Mam and Doctor Bernstein
and I remembered this was the hospital and there were concentration camps and I was still going to die – and then everybody
said how I was – and I said quite well – and they said what a brave
little girl I was in the zapper and that I should have a special little
present – and that it was a special CD player what the nurses had
bought me 'cos they knew I liked the opera – but I couldn't wear it
inside the machine on account of the interference – after a few
days they told me the zapper was not really such a zapper at all –
and in fact it was called an accelerator – which means to go very
fast – but it is for to slow the cancer down – and I sat for hours –
but the cancer never slowed – in fact that the centigrays hardly
stopped it at all – and they said I had to go home for a while.

I started getting even worse than I was – really woozy and
everything and virtually as soon as I had got out of the hospital they

said I had to go back in – this time they said there'd be no more
machines and stuff – but they would give me this special thing
in my arm and that would make me sick and have diarrhoea and all
my hair would fall out – this was the chemicals and such and they
said that if that didn't save me, that was that – so I went and had the
diarrhoea – and they put the thing in my arm – like a tap which
they had all bags and special machines which had these chemicals
that they put in my arm and made me ill – I was feeling quite sickly
and then I had to have this medicine to stop me puking up – it is
quite hard to have the diarrhoea and want to puke up at the same
time because you don't know which one to do first – and this was
called a side-effect – but it effected all over – and I would sit in
the bed with the arm thing and my new CD and then I would poo
myself and my hair all fell out and I was quite weird – then one day
Dad came and he had this hat for me to wear it had a picture
of these opera singers on the front and I wore the hat even though
I was inside – and everyday I was sicker and sicker and I goes
to God – Please God, why are you making me so sickly? – and
I never found out – because he never said – then I was quite
depressed – and my eyebrows fell out.

Doctor Bernstein came to see how I was and he said it must
be horrible having diarrhoea – but I said I didn't mind that
much, and anyway that's what Beethoven had when he wrote his
music – he had diarrhoea and deafness – and he was quite ill a lot of
the time – but he wrote the beautiful music – and the doctor said
how did I know such things and I said someone told me what
looked at my tapes.

Then Doctor Bernstein said there was this man, Job, and he had
a horrible time except he put up with it and he was alright. Doctor
Bernstein said that Job was a Jew too and so was Jesus and so was
all these famous people – and that there was a lot to suffer in the
history of the world – which is true – and one day he came to me
and took off the drip and said that the good news was that my
hair would grow – but the bad news was I was still full of cancer

and there was nothing to be done – all the chemicals and the centi-grays and everything was useless.

When I went home I was in bed a lot and I used to watch everything through the window – and had lots of time to be by myself and think about things and that.

First – when Mam brought me home, then Mam said that I was a brave little girl indeed because of my baldness and everything and that my hair would be growing in soon – but then when there was Dad there and that he was allowed to stay on the sofa down-stairs for every day that I was alive – then I was in bed and then I would have the pills and stuff which is called morphine – and I would be propped so I would look out of the window – then she said that she did hate God and how could he do such a thing to poor Spoonface who was in bed – which was me – only I could hear and everything and Dad said to her for to be philosophical and Mam said that philosophicals could just go away and that she did hate God – as basically God is a bastard – this is what I heard and then I looked up and saw the wind.

MUSIC: *Maria Callas singing 'Voi lo sapete, O mamma' from* Cavalleria Rusticana *by Mascagni*

And when we went home the doctor gave me this book to me – but I can't read so I had to get Mam to read it to me – and then I found all this stuff out – like you had to pray to God – and that this would help get on his good side and even if you did die then he'd look out for you afterwards – and in the book it said there was different ways you can pray – there is like when you get up and sit and say things – that is one way of praying – and then there is like you go to the synagogue and then everybody does it all together and that – and then there is this different way what was invented by these people in Poland quite a while ago – this is when everything you do is a prayer – and you have to do everything you do the best you can because it is not just normal, in fact it is a prayer straight to God – when you smile that is a

prayer – when you talk that's a prayer – and when you walk that's
a prayer – and when you brush your teeth and when you give
someone a kiss – and Mams and Dads when they go to bed that is a
prayer – and when you pray that is a prayer – and when you spit,
when you suck, when you laugh, when you dance, when you
snore – everything you do is a prayer – 'specially what you do when
you meet other people because all the people in the world are in
God's kingdom – and it doesn't even matter if they're Jewish – and
all the animals, all the birds and bees and fishes and swans and
llamas and piglets and worms and trees and buses and cars and
people and that – because when the world was made, God made it
out of magic sparks – everything that there is, was all made of magic
sparks – and all the magic sparks went into things – deep down
and everything has a spark – but it was quite a while ago since it
was made and now the sparks are deep down inside and the whole
point of being alive – the whole point of living is to find the
spark – and when you meet someone and say hello – or if you tell
them a joke or when you say that you love them or try and help
someone or you see someone who is sad or injured or maybe they
have lost all their money or have been battered up or maybe they're
just a bit glum or hungry or you ask the time or maybe they've
missed the train – all these people, all they need is help to find the
spark – and the people what invented this – the Hassid's a long time
ago, when they saw people that were having a chat they saw the
sparks jump in the space in between them – the sparks were
jumping like electricity – sparks God put there – and the sparks
were put there for each other 'cos God wanted people to find
them in each other – and doing this making sparks – this was to
pray – and the old people a long time ago they saw the sparks and
when people met and the sparks jumped right up into the air
from the place they were hiding and they leapt up through the
firmament and through the clouds and past the sun and they
shone over the whole universe – and when people kissed there
were sparks and when people held each other there were sparks and
when they waved as they were going away in a car there would be
sparks and they would all be prayers – they would all be prayers

for the babies and the sad people with cancer – and for the kings
to be good – and the experts to be clever – and all the Mams and
Dads and the cleaning ladies and the milkmen – and if only you
could see the spark then there was a meaning – because what was
the meaning of anything? – if you were going to die, what was the
meaning? – all the trees and the bushes and the famines and wars
and disasters and even pencils or pens – what was the meaning of
all these things? – and the meaning was if you found the spark –
then it would be like electricity – and you would glow like a light
and you would shine like the sparks and that was the meaning – it
wasn't like an answer or a number or any such – it was glow-
ing – it was finding the sparks inside you and setting them free.

This is what it said in this book what the doctor gave me – the
doctor what's Mam was the little girl whose Mam got shot – and it
meant that the meaning that everybody thought was somewhere
else was right here – and all you had to do was do the sparks and
become like a lightbulb – and the meaning wasn't that I was going
to die but that I was still alive – and I could make everybody
shine – the bus boys and the milkmen and Mrs Spud – and
I thought, if I wasn't scared of when I wasn't born why would I be
scared of when I wasn't existed at the other end – you can't feel the
end or touch the end – 'cos it was just nothing – the end of things
is not the problem 'cos there was really no ends to find – that was
the meaning there are no real ends – only middles, and even if I was
at the end I was still in the middle – 'cos it wouldn't know it was
the end then – because it would be ended – so everything is in the
middle – even if it was at the middle of an end – it didn't matter
because I'm in it.

And when I looked to my middle and I saw underneath there
was a belly and bones and muscles and veins and cancer and
intestines but in the middle of the middle was sparks – the sparks
what would save me – the sparks what I could make shine – the
sparks that knew there was no more endings – the sparks what
would be as a huge light in the world and the sparks would fly up
and take me to heaven.

MUSIC: *Maria Callas singing 'Vissi d'arte, vissi d'amore'*
from Tosca *by Puccini*

During the day Mrs Spud comes in and sees me – she makes
me stuff and that and helps out Mam with the laundry and the
cleaning and she makes the house spick and span and that – if I was
to grow up, I would be like Mrs Spud and everyday I would clean
the fridge and the oven and the shelves and the steps out to
the garden and some of the skirting boards, but I would leave the
shelves where nobody looks and everything would be clean.

I asked Mrs Spud where I got my cancer from and she did not
know – I said, I think I might have caught it off God and she said
God does not have cancer as far as we know – I said, maybe he's just
not telling anybody – Mrs Spud says that if God has got cancer
we're all in trouble – I think maybe he has or he has not.

She said she has a son who is a little angel and a husband who is
dead – he had the cancer too – only his was of a difference – she
did weep when she told me about him and how when they were
just children they met and he kissed her on the neck and that – and
on those days that the sun shone forever – she said that the trouble
is when people are around – you forget that they are quite special
and when they are gone it is too late to tell them and you must
always tell them – she said there was nobody like her husband and
that he was a very kind man to her – and when she spoke of
him you could tell as her eyes were sparkly and her breath was
warm – and although he was gone away he was also here – and that
every day they had a little chat – and how was the weather and in
heaven it never rained – she said we would all be there in the
same place one day and maybe I'll get to meet him – I said I didn't
know if I could go to there on account of being Jewish – but
she was sure I would – his name was Mr Spud.

Then I said that I quite liked the rain when it was wet and it
blew so grey on the ground and I would watch from the bed when
the trees would weep and bend in the day – and I saw how the

shed wobbled in the wind – and I would see the cloud for all the silver there was in it – and every day of the rain, the sun even in its little bits made the world spark like diamonds and glisten in the weather – and if I was in heaven there would be no dull to shine out in the sad days – but Mrs Spud said she liked the sun and when she could afford she would go on a nice holiday in Ibiza – although Jimmy – which is her son – would not go on account of the price – which is a shame.

I asked her if she was lonely without poor Mr Spud – she said a bit and that she would lie and remember him whenever – but then again we are not gone – then I said, did she see that there was blackness and she did not – she said there was sadness and stuff but that's what there is – but if you look there is also happiness – like little children having a smile – or someone with a birthday – and even in a graveyard there might be a little butterfly flying round the gravestones – and these are the things what is important – and poor Mr Spud would be sad in heaven if he thought that Mrs Spud didn't look at the day and see that in the trees and in the sky there was a little piece of heaven.

I felt sad for Mrs Spud as she had three hungry mouths to feed – her and Jimmy and someone else – and one day she came into my room to do the hoovering and I had poo'd in my pants and it was a disgusting smell and she cleaned my bum and the bed for me – and I made her a card the next day – and it said 'I love You Mrs Spud' – and she cried – and she cried when she got it – she said, what a lovely card – and I said I did my best considering the crayons I had which was not very many and there was no blue so there was no proper sky – but she said it was quite a beautiful card for a cleaner .

MUSIC: *'Maria Callas singing 'Vissi d'arte, vissi d'amore'
from* Tosca

When you think about dying it is very hard to do – it is to think about what is not – to think about everything there is nothing – to

not be and never to be again – it is even more than emptiness – if
you think of emptiness it is full of nothing and death is more than
this – death is even less than nothing – when you think about
that you will not be here for your breakfast – and that you will
never see Mam or Dad or Mrs Spud – or the telly or hear the sweet
singing opera ladies or feel anything any more – but you won't
feel sad as there will be nothing to feel of – and that is the weird
point – not that there is even anything but there is not even
nothing – and that is death.

Sometimes it is scary – but to think that I'll not be is impossible
because I'm here – and when I'm not here there'll still be cows
and grass and vegetables and radios and telephone machines and
cardiologists and soup tins and cookers and hats and shoes and
Walkmans and Tiny Tears and synagogues and beaches and sun-
shine and walks in the rain and films and music and my coat and
my shoes and cars and underpants and necklaces and my Mam and
Dad and flowers – everywhere there'll be something in the whole
world everything will be full except me – and there isn't even a
hole somewhere where I used to be – and apart from people what
remember me and what I was like there is nothing missing from
when I was here – there is no space in the universe where people
have dropped out – it is all filled in as full as ever – there is nothing
to know, as is everything that there is, is all around us – there is
nothing to know because there it is – in the world everything
is divided – everything divided one from the other one, from the
many – from the mother and from the father – there is day and
night and black and white and all these things but in the very
beginning and in the end – everything will not be divided and
there will be no me or you – there will be no this or that, no little
puppy dogs or anything, there will only be that everything is
the same – and every moment is forever – and it will shine and
it will be everything and nothing – and that is all there is
to know – that all of us will end up being one – and that is
nothing – and it is endless.

MUSIC: *Maria Callas singing 'Ebben? ne andrò lontana'*
from La Wally *by Catalani*

Blessed and lauded, glorified and lifted and exalted and
    enhanced and elevated and praised be the Name
    of the Holy One,
Blessed be he although he is high above all blessings, hymns
    and uplifts that can be voices in this world.
May his name be blessed for ever and ever.

(The Kaddish)

THE END